THE UNITED KINGDOM
AND NUCLEAR DETERRENCE

JEREMY STOCKER

ADELPHI PAPER 386

The International Institute for Strategic Studies

Arundel House | 13–15 Arundel Street | Temple Place | London | WC2R 3DX | UK

ADELPHI PAPER 386

First published February 2007 by **Routledge**
4 Park Square, Milton Park, Abingdon, Oxon, OX14 4RN

for **The International Institute for Strategic Studies**
Arundel House, 13–15 Arundel Street, Temple Place, London, WC2R 3DX, UK
www.iiss.org

Simultaneously published in the USA and Canada by **Routledge**
270 Madison Ave., New York, NY 10016

Routledge is an imprint of Taylor & Francis, an Informa Business

DIRECTOR-GENERAL AND CHIEF EXECUTIVE John Chipman
EDITOR Tim Huxley
MANAGER FOR EDITORIAL SERVICES Ayse Abdullah
ASSISTANT EDITOR Jessica Delaney
PRODUCTION John Buck
COVER IMAGE © Crown Copyright/MOD. Reproduced with the permission of
the Controller of Her Majesty's Stationery Office.

Printed and bound in Great Britain by Bell & Bain Ltd, Thornliebank, Glasgow

British Library Cataloguing in Publication Data
A catalogue record for this book is available from the British Library

Library of Congress Cataloguing in Publication Data

ISBN 978-0-415-43834-6
ISSN 0567-932X

Contents

GLOSSARY

ABM	Anti-ballistic missile
AWE	Atomic Weapons Establishment
BMD	Ballistic missile defence
CASD	Continuous At-Sea Deterrent
CBRN	Chemical, biological, radiological, nuclear
CBW	Chemical and biological weapons
CTBT	Comprehensive Test Ban Treaty
FMCT	Fissile Material Cut-off Treaty
ICBM	Intercontinental Ballistic Missile
IRBM	Intermediate-range ballistic missile
MoD	Ministry of Defence
NPR	Nuclear Posture Review
NPT	Nuclear Non-Proliferation Treaty
NSA	Negative Security Assurance
NWS	Nuclear-Weapon States
PSI	Proliferation Security Initiative
PWR	Pressurised Water Reactor
RNAD	Royal Naval Armament Depot
RRW	Reliable replacement warhead
RV	Re-entry vehicle
SDR	Strategic Defence Review
SIB	Submarine industrial base
SLBM	Submarine-launched ballistic missile
SLCM	Submarine-launched cruise missile
SSBN	Nuclear-powered ballistic missile submarine
SSN	Nuclear-powered attack submarine
WMD	Weapons of mass destruction

'It would be dangerously wrong to suppose that the end of the Cold War means an end of nuclear danger.'

McGeorge Bundy, William J. Crowe, Jr, and Sidney D. Drell,
Reducing Nuclear Danger: The Road Away from the Brink
(New York: Council on Foreign Relations, 1993), p. 2.

'This is a second nuclear age.'

Colin S. Gray, *The Second Nuclear Age*
(Boulder, CO: Lynne Rienner, 1999), p. 1.

'The Government believes that now, as in the Cold War ... an independent British nuclear deterrent is an essential part of our insurance against the uncertainties and risks of the future.'

Tony Blair, Foreword to Government White Paper,
The Future of the United Kingdom's Nuclear Deterrent,
Cm 6994 (London: TSO, December 2006).

INTRODUCTION

As the third country to develop nuclear weapons, Britain became the world's first 'small' nuclear power. Most of its nuclear history has been determined by the need to help to deter a hostile, nuclear-armed superpower, the Soviet Union. Possession of a nuclear deterrent provided the 'ultimate guarantee' of national survival during the Cold War. It also preserved some element of Great Power status and a means of exercising influence with its all-important principal ally, the United States.

Now that the Cold War has ended and the Soviet Union is no more, Britain's security is assured to a degree probably unprecedented in its history, notwithstanding the lethal irritations of Islamist terrorism and regional challenges to British interests abroad. Whatever role nuclear weapons may have today, it is not the purpose for which they were first acquired and then maintained for nearly 40 years.

The Cold War ended as the United Kingdom was bringing a new strategic nuclear system into service: the *Trident* missiles purchased from the United States were to carry British warheads and were themselves to be carried in four British-designed and built submarines, the *Vanguard*-class. The changed strategic environment might have called for a reappraisal of the UK's nuclear requirements, but there were no pressing procurement decisions to prompt such a comprehensive review. British official policy remained conservative on nuclear matters.[1]

Substantial reductions were made in Britain's holdings of nuclear warheads and their delivery systems, but these mainly concerned tactical and theatre weapons. The strategic nuclear deterrent remained practically unchanged from Cold War-era plans and in 1996 was still considered the 'ultimate guarantee of our national security'.[2] Two years later, *Trident* was the UK's sole nuclear-weapon system and had taken on a largely undefined 'sub-strategic' role in addition to its original strategic task. The fourth *Vanguard*-class submarine, HMS *Vengeance*, became operational in 2001, thus completing the original *Trident* programme.

Nuclear matters remained in the news and on the political agenda, but owing to events abroad rather than at home. India and Pakistan both conducted nuclear-weapon tests in 1998. North Korea's weapons programme has been a source of international concern for more than a decade, and the country attempted a nuclear test in 2006. Much diplomatic attention and media speculation has been devoted to Iran's nuclear programme, which is ostensibly for civil purposes, and possible American or Israeli attacks aimed at bringing it to a halt.[3] Meanwhile, in 1995 the Nuclear Non-Proliferation Treaty (NPT) was extended indefinitely, and further strengthened in 2000. Britain's nuclear capability remained, as the *Economist* put it, 'not just out of sight, but also out of mind'.[4]

A Labour government took power in Britain in 1997 and completed a Strategic Defence Review (SDR) the following year. It claimed to have conducted a 'rigorous re-examination of our deterrence requirements',[5] but was already committed to the retention of *Trident*, still regarding it as the 'ultimate guarantee'.[6] The SDR made a small reduction in the number of deployed warheads and made several aspects of nuclear policy more transparent, but did not lead to substantial changes. Britain's stockpile of fewer than 200 warheads represents about 1.4% of the world total of nuclear weapons.[7]

In 2003 the oldest British nuclear-armed submarine, *Vanguard*, was only 10 years old and *Vengeance* was almost brand new. It came, therefore, as a considerable surprise to many when a new Defence White Paper announced that 'decisions on whether to replace Trident are not needed [in] this Parliament but are likely to be required in the next one'.[8] Whether the government intended to initiate a new public debate on such a politically sensitive subject or not, this simple statement certainly had that effect.

In September 2005 the Ministry of Defence (MoD) insisted that 'no decisions on any replacement for the Trident system have been taken, either in principle or in detail ... decisions ... are still some way off'.[9] A little over a year later, those decisions had been taken: 'we have ... decided to take the steps necessary to sustain a credible deterrent capability in the 2020s and beyond ... We have ... decided to maintain our nuclear deterrent by building a new class of submarines'.[10]

Major public decisions on the nuclear deterrent come around roughly every 20 years and are usually controversial.[11] Significantly, the British strategic deterrent has always been known by the name of its delivery system rather than by those of the nuclear warheads themselves. The delivery system is considerably more expensive than any warhead and the periodic debates have usually been prompted by the need to make decisions about it.

This time, the government's resolve is to extend the operational life of the existing system for another 20 years or so beyond the early 2020s when it would otherwise go out of service. The nuclear deterrent comprises four main elements: the warheads; the *Trident* missiles; the *Vanguard*-class submarines; and the supporting shore infrastructure.[12] Three of these elements, the warheads, missiles and infrastructure, are to be upgraded and renewed. Only the submarines are actually to be replaced. The deterrent will essentially remain in its present form (though with a reduction in warhead and, possibly, submarine numbers) and will continue to operate in the same way as at present. The money to be spent will, therefore, maintain the status quo.

The sum of money entailed is, in absolute terms, considerable: £15–20 billion, spread over a 15-year period.[13] It could have major significance for the defence budget as a whole. But an average of around £1bn per annum is somewhat trivial in relation to overall government spending of over £500bn per year and the intrinsic importance of a country having, or not having, nuclear weapons. As no change of nuclear status is involved, one might question why there should be any controversy or debate at all.[14] However, the intention to spend this kind of money does require parliamentary and public scrutiny. As Britain's nuclear status is being determined for another generation, there is both an opportunity and a need for a thorough-going review of British nuclear-weapons policy. So far, though, this has not occurred.

The decisions being made by the British government about the future of the nuclear deterrent are, for the first time, being taken outside the Cold War context within which *Trident* was originally procured. That does not mean that British nuclear-weapons policy-making can start afresh. The Cold War has left a physical legacy in the form of the *Trident* system and also, just as importantly, a half-century of experience of living in a nuclear-armed world. There is a legacy of policy and doctrine in nuclear matters deriving from the Cold War. Some, though not all, of it is of enduring relevance, not just to the UK but also to emerging small nuclear powers, which have to grapple with issues of deterrence postures, targeting strategies, credibility and vulnerability, technological challenges and resource constraints similar to those which Britain has faced for over 60 years.

The most fundamental nuclear question is whether to remain a nuclear-weapon state at all. There have always been plenty of vocal proponents of unilateral nuclear disarmament, to an extent that is unique to the UK. Other nuclear-weapon states have never engaged in the protracted debate about nuclear status that has been a feature of British politics, on and off, since the late 1950s. The current British government has made its position clear. While re-iterating a long-term aspiration for a nuclear-free world, it believes that:

> the continuing risk from the proliferation of nuclear weapons, and the certainty that a number of other countries will retain substantial nuclear arsenals, mean that our minimum nuclear deterrent capability, currently represented by Trident, is likely to remain a necessary element of our security.[15]

The decision in favour of retaining the UK's nuclear weapons is probably politically inevitable and, more importantly, is the right one given Britain's likely future strategic circumstances.

If the UK is to retain a nuclear deterrent it must consider what and how it is to deter. Britain no longer needs to ward off a threat from the Soviet Union. But it does live in a world in which nuclear weapons are becoming more widely spread, even if less numerous.[16] The 'second nuclear age' is less threatening than the first, but it is also a less certain and more unpredictable phase than the Cold War. It could, one day, be succeeded by a third nuclear age if a major, direct nuclear threat to the UK were to re-emerge.[17] However, in the absence of a known nuclear opponent, establishing an appropriate and credible deterrence posture is, at best, problematic. But it is too important to ignore if the deterrent is to be effective. A so-called 'existential' deterrent that relies simply on the sheer awfulness of nuclear weapons is most likely to deter itself. 'Non-proliferation' is essentially a diplomatic process that seeks to prevent the further spread of nuclear weapons. Its principal, though not only, instrument is the 1968 NPT, which legitimises the UK's nuclear status as one of five acknowledged nuclear-weapon states, but also commits those states to eventual complete disarmament. Deterrence, which requires the retention of nuclear weapons, seems naturally to be at odds with non-proliferation, which tries to limit and ultimately abolish their possession. Britain, which actively pursues both deterrence and non-proliferation, is often accused of hypocrisy – keeping nuclear weapons for itself while trying to deny them to others. But the two are not, or should not be, mutually exclusive. Non-proliferation policies try to reduce the scale of potential threats which may need to be deterred. Pending the realisation of a nuclear-free world,[18] deterrence and non-proliferation work together to maintain security in a nuclear-armed world.

The future shape of Britain's nuclear forces has recently been decided by the British government. Despite the superficial attractions of some alternative options, a life-extension for the *Trident* system and the construction of new submarines are the best means of meeting the UK's needs.

It has taken the British government just three years from first raising the issue to decide on the future of the British nuclear deterrent. It has allowed another 17 years in which to bring the first of the new submarines into service,[19] by which time a further decision will have to have been made on a future delivery system. The December 2006 White Paper is perhaps the most comprehensive statement by any British government of its nuclear deterrent policy. The aim of this study is to provide an independent examination of Britain's decisions within the relevant historical, policy and strategic contexts.

CHAPTER ONE

A Nuclear Legacy

On 3 October 1952 Britain detonated its first atomic device and became the world's third nuclear-weapon power. Britain was actually the first country seriously to investigate the possibility of producing an atomic weapon utilising the enormous power of nuclear fission.[1] The Maud Committee, set up in April 1940, reported the following year and initiated a research and development programme which was soon, however, subsumed into the larger Anglo-American *Manhattan Project*.[2]

Wartime cooperation was ended in 1946 when the US Congress passed Senator Brien McMahon's Atomic Energy Act, largely in ignorance of the extent of Britain's contribution to the *Manhattan Project*. In January 1947, a small Cabinet committee chaired by Prime Minister Clement Attlee decided in secret to proceed with developing a British atomic bomb.[3] At about the same time, the Air Staff issued operational requirements for medium jet bombers – the V-bombers – which were to deliver the new weapons.

For one of the Second World War's victorious 'big three', the decision to acquire the most powerful weapon system seemed, then and in retrospect, natural. Britain's economic weakness and its diminished military strength in relation to its two wartime allies made atomic weapons an attractive 'leveller'. With the future of the Anglo-American relationship in some doubt and the emerging Soviet threat increasingly apparent, the bomb offered a way to maintain Britain's status in relation to the United States, and its security against the Soviet Union. While pursuing a national capability, the UK simultaneously sought to restore its atomic relationship with the United States. The latter's commitment to the defence of Western Europe would be the best, and perhaps only, way to secure Britain in the face of the Soviet Union. Thus the pattern for British nuclear-weapons policy for the next 40 years was set.

Britain acquired an operational nuclear capability in 1956 when the first V-bombers armed with the *Blue Danube* free-fall fission weapon became operational. Even before the UK acquired an operational *deterrent*, a policy of nuclear *deterrence* was firmly established as the only possible counter to the threat of nuclear attack.[4] The 1952 Global Strategy Paper set out the basic stance:

> Since no effective defence against atomic attack is in sight, the primary deterrent must be the knowledge on the part of the Kremlin that any aggression on their part will involve immediate retaliation ... with the atomic weapon.[5]

It was also realised that the initial capability would be just that. The atomic breakthrough of 1945 was followed by two further, perhaps more significant, developments. Thermonuclear (fusion) weapons produced several orders of magnitude of greater explosive power and ushered in the nuclear age in a way that modest numbers of relatively low-yield fission weapons perhaps had not. Ballistic missiles offered a way of delivering them that could not (unlike manned bombers) be intercepted. By the late 1950s the Soviets had fusion weapons and ballistic missiles. Britain had neither, and its new deterrent capability began to look obsolescent even as it entered service.

In response to this emerging shortfall in nuclear-weapons capability, in 1953–54 the British government took two related decisions. One was to develop a fusion weapon, or 'H-bomb', and the other to build an intermediate-range ballistic missile (IRBM) called *Blue Streak* to deliver it. The 1957 Defence White Paper built on earlier thinking, further emphasising the nuclear deterrent at the expense of conventional forces, including an end to conscription.

After several years of diplomatic lobbying, nuclear collaboration with the United States was partially restored in 1954 with Congressional passage of another Atomic Energy Act, which permitted a limited bilateral exchange of information. This was followed in 1956 by a US initiative to station American IRBMs in Britain to help to counter the growing Soviet nuclear capability. Agreement was reached in 1957–58 for the basing of 60 US *Thor* missiles in the UK, under a 'dual-key' arrangement whereby the consent of both governments was required to authorise their launch. The missiles and their nuclear warheads were supplied by the US, but operated by RAF personnel with an American authentication controller. Highly vulnerable to pre-emptive attack, they did not long remain in service and all were withdrawn by 1963.[6]

Anglo-American cooperation was also intensifying in the field of nuclear targeting, now that the UK had some operational capability. The real breakthrough in cooperation, however, followed the British *Grapple* series of thermonuclear tests between May 1957 and September 1958.[7] These coincided with the Soviet launch of the *Sputnik* satellite and what Washington perceived as a 'missile gap'. These developments gave the US a real incentive for extensive strategic cooperation with its only proven nuclear ally, the UK. The 1958 Agreement for Cooperation on the Uses of Atomic Energy for Mutual Defence Purposes[8] finally amended the McMahon Act and set the pattern for close and exclusive nuclear cooperation between the two countries that has endured to this day. In particular, the agreement allows the UK to draw on American warhead designs,[9] though these are always 'anglicised' and the weapons built in Britain. This access to US warhead designs was important because American delivery systems require warheads designed to fit them.

The first British fusion bomb (the one-megaton *Yellow Sun* Mk 2) became operational in 1961 and armed an improved series of V-bombers. This capability was still, however, a free-fall bomb delivered by a subsonic manned bomber. It was increasingly vulnerable to pre-emptive attack from Soviet missiles while still on the ground and, once airborne, had to penetrate extensive Soviet air defences. A pessimistic report in June 1961 assessed the UK's deterrent as just 1% effective – an assessment that was not widely circulated.[10] The *Blue Steel* Mk 1 stand-off powered bomb which entered service two years later only marginally improved the situation as it had a range of only 100 miles, was unreliable and took considerable time to prepare.

As well as an extended range *Blue Steel* Mk 2 (later cancelled), the solution was to have been *Blue Streak*. But this was a liquid-fuelled IRBM launched from fixed silos. Though impervious to Soviet defences once launched it was likely to prove as vulnerable to pre-emptive strike as the V-bombers. Accordingly, it was cancelled in April 1960. Britain did not have the resources to develop several delivery systems simultaneously and, with the demise of the land-based IRBM, had to turn to the Americans.

There was already some interest in Britain in the US Navy's new submarine-launched ballistic missile (SLBM) *Polaris*. But the Royal Navy's priorities for the moment lay elsewhere (in aircraft carriers, in particular), while the strategic deterrent was central to the RAF's Cold War role. The American *Skybolt* air-launched ballistic missile was selected to replace *Blue Streak*.

From the beginning there were doubts about the wisdom of this reliance on the United States, not least because it was never certain that the Americans would persist with the *Skybolt* project. Moreover, *Skybolt* could do no more than improve the performance of the V-bomber force and thereby extend its operational life. It did not solve the problem of what should eventually replace the V-bombers.

Just two years later, in November 1962, the Americans did indeed cancel *Skybolt* on cost and performance grounds. This caused a minor crisis in Anglo-American relations which demonstrated how reliant the British had become on the US. *Polaris* was now the only possible option as both manned aircraft and land-based missiles were too vulnerable in a small country relatively close to the Soviet Union. The *Skybolt* cancellation was followed quickly by a long-planned Anglo-American conference in Nassau in December 1962. The future of the British deterrent now topped the agenda and the Americans were persuaded to support their key ally in maintaining its nuclear capability.

A sea-based deterrent

Almost by default, after all other possibilities had been exhausted, Britain finally got the one nuclear delivery system, *Polaris*, which met the needs of a small, densely populated island state in straitened economic conditions, even if it did have to be purchased, on favourable terms, from another country.

As a result of the Nassau agreement, the strategic nuclear deterrent was committed to NATO as a contribution to the Alliance's overall deterrent strategy, except 'where Her Majesty's government may decide that supreme national interests are at stake'. As the use of nuclear weapons could only be contemplated under such circumstances this subsequently oft-repeated statement was little more than a diplomatic nicety, though some targeting plans were coordinated through NATO.

Although the missiles themselves were purchased from the United States, their warheads (three per missile) were British designed and built. The submarines were also British, created essentially by inserting a missile compartment in the middle of the existing *Valiant*-class nuclear-powered attack submarine (SSN) design. Less than six years after the British government committed itself to *Polaris*, the first submarine, *Resolution*, was at sea. This was a remarkable achievement.[11] In 1969 the Royal Navy took over the strategic deterrent role from the RAF, whose nuclear-capable aircraft were reduced in number and re-assigned to 'theatre' nuclear and conventional roles. The 'deterrent gap'[12] seemed to have been closed.

Polaris did not, however, resolve all Britain's nuclear dilemmas. By now the Soviet Union was known to be developing anti-ballistic missile (ABM) systems. While it seemed unlikely that these could pose a significant challenge to the huge strategic arsenal of the United States, for the UK it was a different matter. The previously anti-*Polaris* Labour government, led by Harold Wilson, had decided to retain the strategic deterrent, but as a token gesture cancelled a planned fifth submarine in January 1965. With four boats, just a single submarine with 16 missiles could be guaranteed to be on station at all times, though often there were two on patrol. The three warheads of a *Polaris* missile separated by only about 10 miles after detaching from the missile and could be destroyed by a single exo-atmospheric megaton-range nuclear burst.[13] One senior MoD official later judged that 'the deployment of the Russian ABM system was not a minor irritant to a country with such a limited deterrent force; it necessitated a major reconsideration of strategic thinking'.[14] Once again, the credibility of the deterrent system was in doubt before it even entered service.

There was a particular difficulty with the Soviet ABM system, as it protected Moscow and an area of several hundred thousand square kilometres around it. For Britain's relatively small deterrent against the Soviet Union to be effective, it had to threaten 'unacceptable damage'. This was the so-called 'Moscow criterion'.[15] Though other targeting options were often considered, it became the consistent view within the British government that only the ability to hit the Soviet capital lent Britain's limited force the required deterrent effect.

The 1972 ABM Treaty, of which the UK was not a signatory, and the amended text of 1974 limited each superpower to just one ABM site with 100 interceptors. This was of critical importance to the UK, as it meant widespread missile defences which could completely negate the small British deterrent would not be deployed. However, it also meant that as the Soviets chose to defend Moscow, the existing *Polaris* force was inadequate.[16]

After protracted study, it was decided to modify the *Polaris* 'front-end'. Two warheads on each missile were made more stealthy and 'hardened' to resist the effects of a nuclear interception. The third warhead was sacrificed for a penetration aid carrier which manoeuvred in space to deploy chaff and around 40 warhead-like decoys. Though drawing on some US work and facilities, this *Chevaline* system was an essentially British technical success. It entered into service in 1982 and extended the effective operational life of *Polaris* well into the 1990s.[17] *Chevaline* also left two enduring legacies for British nuclear-weapons policy. It gave the UK a particular insight into the tasks both of building, and overcoming, effective ballistic missile defence (BMD) systems. It also demonstrated the financial and operational penalties of developing and operating a unique system rather than staying in tune with the Americans.[18]

Even before *Chevaline*-modified *Polaris* missiles were in service, it was necessary once again to consider their eventual replacement. The benefits of a submarine-based deterrent were by now widely accepted. Accordingly, in January 1979, Labour Prime Minister James Callaghan (Wilson's successor) sounded out the Jimmy Carter administration regarding the availability of the USN's new system, *Trident*. The answer was positive.[19] A formal decision and request was, however, left to the Conservative government led by Margaret Thatcher which came to power in May 1979.

Independence, interdependence and dependence

The physical component of the UK nuclear deterrent during the period before *Trident* changed substantially. But the underlying strategic rationale and the deterrent policy manifest consistent themes, many of which endure today. At the heart of British nuclear-weapons policy has been a complex relationship between independence, interdependence and dependence – all of them in relation to the United States. Indeed, one can argue that while the UK nuclear deterrent was originally aimed operationally at the Soviet Union, strategically it has always been aimed at the United States. Put another way, it was Britain's relationship with its principal ally rather than with its principal enemy that most influenced its nuclear stance.

The 'independence' of the deterrent performed several functions. Particularly in the earlier years, it was seen as a mark of continuing international status as a Great Power.[20] Ernest Bevin, who served as foreign secretary between 1945 and 1951, put it succinctly: 'We've got to have this thing over here, whatever it costs. We've got to have the bloody Union Jack on top of it.'[21] Once Britain had a deterrent, Winston Churchill's son Randolph, himself a member of Parliament, said in 1958, 'we are a Great Power again'.[22] In later years, when the reality of superpower bipolarity was all too evident, nuclear status at least differentiated the UK from other second-tier powers such as Germany and Japan.

More specifically, a British nuclear capability was expected to act as a hedge against the failure of the American nuclear guarantee of Europe – or at least against a Soviet perception that that guarantee was no longer credible, because of the vulnerability of the United States.[23] This led to the rationale that a 'second centre of decision-making' would complicate Soviet calculations; Moscow would need to take British, as well as American, actions into account.

As Avery Goldstein of the University of Pennsylvania put it, 'Britain decided on an independent nuclear deterrent as the security insurance it needed and could afford.'[24] Independence, however, could be no substitute for interdependence with allies. The nuclear umbrella provided by NATO and the US always remained Britain's preferred counter to the huge Soviet threat. Britain's own capability was a way of demonstrating to Washington that the UK was 'pulling its weight' and that its views and interests should be taken seriously. A UK force contribution would enable it to influence US nuclear plans and actions. For their part, the Americans were willing to cooperate on nuclear matters only when the UK had demonstrated both will and capability. British nuclear policy has, therefore, always been heavily influenced by 'what the Americans will think'.[25]

Nuclear-weapons cooperation with the US, once re-established after 1958, enabled the UK to continue to develop and produce its own warheads but now with the benefit of American knowledge, access to American facilities and more cheaply than under the hitherto fully independent programme. Access to the Nevada nuclear-weapons test site was particularly important when atmospheric tests were banned by the 1963 Partial Test Ban Treaty.[26]

Nevertheless, interdependence inevitably implied a degree of dependence, for Britain could only ever be the junior partner in this relationship. The importance of the US nuclear guarantee to Europe was clear. But it was in the provision of a delivery system that Britain became most dependent on the United States. Britain's economic and technological base proved inadequate to support a first-class nuclear delivery system, and against the Soviet Union only a first-class system would do. Successive British governments have simply not been prepared to allocate the resources necessary to develop and build Britain's own delivery systems, as successive French governments have. This practical dependence has been sharply at odds with the notional 'independence' of the deterrent, though Britain has always emphasised independence of use rather than independence of procurement.[27]

Cooperation with the United States and hostility towards the Soviet Union led Britain into a policy of 'minimum deterrence', or 'small but sufficient'.[28] For the deterrent to have the desired effect on the Russians it was necessary at least to imply that Moscow was the main target.

Throughout the Cold War, strategic deterrence was not the only function of British nuclear weapons. A more limited 'theatre' role was filled by the WE 177 free-fall bomb and its predecessors, and WE 177s were deployed for tactical use as nuclear depth bombs for anti-submarine operations. Some small US warheads were deployed by British troops as artillery shells and on short-range *Lance* missiles under another dual-key arrangement.[29] All of these weapons were withdrawn from service after the end of the Cold War.

One source suggests that the total number of British nuclear warheads peaked at 410 at the end of the 1960s, around the time that *Polaris* replaced the V-bombers in the strategic role. A total of 1,200 weapons were built between 1952 and 2001, roughly the same as in France but only a small fraction of the number acquired by the United States and the Soviet Union.[30] The total British 'megatonnage' (a very early-Cold War concept) probably peaked in the mid-1960s at up to 230MT,[31] compared to less than 20MT today. Britain carried out 44 nuclear tests in total, the last on 26 November 1991. From 1962 onwards these were all conducted at the Nevada test site.[32]

Establishing the cost of British nuclear weapons, up to and including the present *Trident* system, is difficult. For example, should the cost of the V-bombers be included? It could be argued instead that with only conventional munitions available, Britain would have needed many *more* aircraft to have similar strategic impact. Should the cost of forces allocated to protect the deterrent be part of the total, or would these conventional forces have been required in any case? Most have been dual-tasked anyway. Nonetheless, by including just nuclear weapons and their delivery systems, one study estimates a total, at 2004 prices, of around £50bn, or an average of £1bn per annum over the last half century.[33] In light of the significance of nuclear weapons this does not seem a disproportionate cost. The proportion of the total defence budget spent on nuclear weapons has generally been well below 5%.

The acquisition of *Trident*

In the late 1970s, with *Chevaline* still under development, the Labour government of the time began to consider what should eventually replace it.[34] Two conclusions emerged. One was that the Moscow Criteria might be less important in future as attention was also now being given to the next nine largest Soviet cities, notwithstanding the imminent entry into service of the Moscow-oriented *Chevaline*. Second, the American *Trident* SLBM was the preferred replacement system. The decision to proceed on this basis was taken by Thatcher's Conservative government in 1980. *Trident* offered two key advantages over alternative systems. Like *Polaris/Chevaline* it was, barring an unforeseen breakthrough in Soviet anti-submarine capabilities, invulnerable prior to launch. It would also minimise technological and financial risks by maintaining commonality with the United States. The need for such commonality was a lesson learned from the protracted and expensive, if ultimately successful, *Chevaline* programme.

The government did examine submarine-launched cruise missiles (SLCMs). Individually these were much cheaper and still benefited from the submarine's invulnerability. But as each SLCM carried a single warhead and might be vulnerable to Soviet air defences, it was calculated that the UK would need to purchase 800 missiles and 11 missile-firing submarines to have the same deterrent effect as four new SSBNs with *Trident*.[35]

In 1980, the US government agreed to sell *Trident* with its multiple independently targeted re-entry vehicles (RVs) under the same terms as the 1963 Polaris Sales Agreement. The UK was originally to have purchased the original C4 version of *Trident*, which could be launched from submarines of about the same size as the existing *Polaris* boats, though owing to their age these would need to be replaced anyway. However, the US Navy soon decided to move on to a new, larger D5 version. In order to maintain future commonality, in 1982 the British government decided to purchase the newer version at somewhat greater initial cost.[36]

Trident C4 could carry eight warheads in Mk 4 RVs, each independently targetable (unlike *Polaris*). This implied a theoretical maximum of 128 warheads per 16-missile submarine (compared to 32 with *Chevaline*). In order to achieve the same deterrent effect rather fewer than 128 were required, though a large number of 'bodies' were still needed in order to overcome Soviet defences.

The larger *Trident* D5 can carry either eight larger Mk 5 RVs or 12 smaller Mk 4s. Britain had no need for the Mk 5, and the government stated in 1982 that, despite its greater capacity, the D5 in UK service would carry no more warheads than the C4 would have done.[37] In fact, it was never planned to carry more than an *average* of six warheads per missile, leaving the remaining 'inert' RVs to act as decoys. Additionally, after development of *Chevaline* was completed, 'generic' research into other decoys continued which could, if required, have maintained Britain's ability to penetrate improved Soviet missile defences. The larger number of warheads carried by *Trident* compared to *Polaris/Chevaline* was also justified by reference to these defences.[38] Nonetheless, *Trident* D5 was 'over-specified' for the UK's 'minimum deterrence' needs, but it was ordered because it was available at the time and provided, crucially, long-term commonality with the US.

The first of the new *Trident* submarines, HMS *Vanguard*, entered service in 1994 and the last *Polaris* submarine was decommissioned two years later. At 2005 prices, the total acquisition cost a little under £15bn,[39] or an average of £750 million per annum over the 20-year period from the decision to acquire *Trident* until the fourth submarine entered service. Unusually for a major weapons-acquisition programme, *Trident* entered service on time and under budget.[40] Running costs of the force vary between 2–4% of the annual defence budget.[41]

The Cold War was over before the first *Trident* submarine went to sea. Even as the new system was entering into service, Britain made substantial reductions in its nuclear armaments, reflecting both the end of animosity with Russia and, for a time, a perceived reduction in nuclear salience. First to go were the maritime weapons, both depth bombs and *Sea Harrier*-delivered WE 177s. In 1993 Britain withdrew from an Anglo-French air-to-surface missile programme which would have replaced the free-fall WE 177s on the RAF's *Tornado* bomber force. Battlefield nuclear weapons, mainly those held under dual-key arrangements with the United States, had all gone by the same year.

At the end of 1993, Defence Secretary Malcolm Rifkind announced yet more reductions. The WE 177 would be phased out entirely by 1998, when *Trident* would assume a 'sub-strategic' role in addition to strategic deterrence. The declared maximum number of warheads carried by each submarine was reduced from 128 to 96 – though it had actually never been the intention to carry more than the lower number. Rifkind also said that the total explosive power carried in a *Trident* submarine would be not much changed from that of *Polaris*.[42] The latter carried 32 200KT warheads, implying about 60 warheads for *Trident*, the warheads for which are similar to the American W 76, which has a yield of about 100KT.[43] It was later revealed that on her first patrol in 1994, HMS *Vanguard* deployed with 'slightly fewer' than 60 warheads and that, on subsequent patrols, submarines 'typically deployed' with 60.[44]

After Labour returned to power in 1997, the new government's SDR, while re-iterating a commitment to a nuclear deterrent, made still further reductions. The number of warheads to be carried now came down to 48, with the government at pains to emphasise that this represented about two-thirds of the explosive power of a *Chevaline*-armed submarine.[45] Greater accuracy and multiple targeting, however, meant that the destructive, as opposed to explosive, power was little changed from *Chevaline*.

Fewer warheads in turn implied that fewer missiles would be required and, accordingly, the total planned purchase of *Trident* missiles was reduced from 65 to 58, of which six had already been test-fired during submarine work ups.[46] The number of 'operationally available' warheads was also reduced, from 300 to fewer than 200. Missiles were 'de-targeted' and now required at least hours rather than the previous 15 minutes' notice to fire.

By the end of the 1990s Britain had just a single nuclear delivery system for the first time since the 1950s.[47] It was also the first nuclear-armed state to rely solely on a submarine platform.[48] The cumulative effect of the post-Cold War reductions was to leave the UK with just 1.5% of the world's strategic nuclear warheads.[49] Paradoxically, however, cuts in American nuclear weapons stationed in Europe meant that British and French weapons between them represented about half of the NATO total, compared to around 10% in the 1970s and 1980s. As Bruno Tertrais wrote in 1999, 'Europe's nuclear weight is thus now much greater, in relative terms, than it was during the Cold War. British and French nuclear weapons are no longer in the shadow of a colossal nuclear presence.'[50]

Possibly more significant than the reductions in missile and warhead numbers was the formulation of a 'sub-strategic' role for *Trident*. The concept was mentioned as early as November 1991, by the then-defence secretary, Tom King.[51] At that time, however, it was still planned to retain an air-launched nuclear capability which would have fulfilled the role. By 1993, however, the MoD had decided that the future air-launched missile was not a significantly high enough priority, so that once the WE 177 was retired it would 'exploit the flexibility and capability of Trident to provide the vehicle for both sub-strategic and strategic aspects of deterrence'.[52] This function was confirmed in the 1998 SDR. However, despite being a good deal more forthcoming on nuclear matters than most previous defence reviews, it had only this to say: 'The credibility of deterrence ... depends on retaining an option for a limited strike that would not automatically lead to a full scale nuclear exchange. Unlike Polaris and Chevaline, Trident must also be capable of performing this "sub-strategic" role.'[53] The British government has never elaborated on the configuration of *Trident* for sub-strategic use, nor how it might be employed. In the December 2006 White Paper, no mention was made of a 'sub-strategic' role. Instead, the ability to vary the number and yield of warheads was linked to credible deterrence of smaller nuclear threats.[54]

As defence analyst Michael Codner has pointed out, 'any deployment or use of a long-range missile-fired nuclear weapon is strategic with a capital "S"'.[55] Many commentators believe that sub-strategic means much the same as the French pre-strategic – a means of firing a 'warning shot' in response to an aggressor's first use of nuclear weapons, or posing a limited and, therefore, credible deterrent threat in the face of small-scale regional nuclear capabilities. This is sub-strategic only in the sense that it does not entail a large-scale Cold War-type nuclear exchange with Russia.

Some facts are known. *Trident* is not a 'tactical' weapon for use on the battlefield.[56] The MoD no longer sees any role for such weapons. The sub-strategic role does not entail a new warhead, but the UK does have a choice of yields for the existing *Trident* warhead.[57] Reduced yields could be obtained by detonating only the un-boosted or boosted fission trigger of the warhead, and using the fusion stage only for the full strategic configuration. This might give a choice of around 1KT, 10KT or 100KT yields.[58] The MoD has not confirmed that a sub-strategic missile carries only a single warhead, but it has never contradicted this widespread assumption.[59] It is certainly difficult to conceive of a sub-strategic use of a multiple-warhead missile.

Trident today

In 2007, the UK's strategic deterrent comprises four 16,000-tonne nuclear-powered ballistic missile-firing submarines (SSBNs), *Vanguard*, *Victorious*, *Vigilant* and *Vengeance*, commissioned in 1994, 1995, 1998 and 2001 respectively. The boats are British designed and built, and differ substantially from their US counterparts. They have a design life of 25 years.[60] Beginning in 2002 they are being fitted with a new reactor core ('Core H'), which eliminates the need to refuel them during their remaining service lives.[61]

Although each submarine can carry 16 *Trident* D5 missiles, they usually deploy with fewer – probably about 12,[62] though the government declines to confirm the exact number.[63] *Trident* is a three-stage, solid-fuel, inertially guided missile with a range, according to payload, of between 6,500km and 12,000km.[64] Britain has 'title' to 58 missiles, part of a jointly managed common pool. They are not leased, as suggested by some commentators. Ten from this total were allocated for tests, of which the majority have already been fired, and an additional four are spares, leaving 44[65] available for operational deployment.

In contrast to its reticence on the number of *missiles* deployed, the government has repeatedly stated that each submarine carries 48 *warheads* on patrol.[66] Perhaps significantly, this figure was changed to 'up to' 48 in the 2006 White Paper.[67] Some of the missiles, probably a majority, will carry a full 'strategic' load of several full-yield warheads – up to six per missile, but with scope for a variable 'lean/rich' mix of inert re-entry vehicles and 'live' warheads. Other missiles carry a single reduced-yield 'sub-strategic' warhead. These may not carry other RVs, in which case they will have a greater range than the 'strategic' weapons. A typical 'load-out' might, therefore, comprise nine missiles with five warheads each and a further three missiles with a single reduced-yield warhead, for a total of 48. This composition is purely speculative, however.

Just a single submarine is maintained on patrol to form the 'Continuous At-Sea Deterrent' (CASD). Under current plans for the submarines, this can be maintained at least until 2019.[68] Control of the deterrent is purely national,[69] and the UK does not, as is sometimes alleged, require any US-supplied data to target the missiles.[70] Notice to fire has nominally been reduced to several days, and missiles have been 'de-targeted'.

The UK has less than 200 'operationally available' warheads in total at any time,[71] though the use of this phrase suggests that more warheads are held in reserve, or are undergoing maintenance. The December 2006 White Paper announced a further 20% cut to 160 warheads plus a reserve.[72]

Some high-readiness conventional forces are still allocated to protection of the deterrent, though fewer than in the past. Most are dual-tasked to other commitments. They include two SSNs, a frigate and several *Nimrod* maritime patrol aircraft.[73]

As Michael Clarke of King's College London succinctly put it, 'the United Kingdom finds itself with a small, highly potent nuclear force composed of the best boats, missiles and warheads currently available in the world'.[74] Colin Gray, perhaps less charitably, calls it 'the gentler, kinder, Blairite nuclear deterrent'.[75]

The three components of the operational deterrent – submarines, missiles and warheads – are supported by a substantial onshore infrastructure. All of Britain's nuclear submarines were built by BAE Systems at Barrow-in-Furness, Cumbria. They are refitted at the Devonport dockyard near Plymouth, and operated from HM Naval Base Clyde at Faslane, a few miles north of Glasgow. This dispersal of functions for what is now a modest submarine force (four SSBNs and eight SSNs) is due in part to a historical legacy and, in part, to particular physical limitations at each of the three sites. For example, *Trident* submarines cannot get in or out of Barrow when fully loaded, and then only under restrictive tidal conditions. Devonport lacks the appropriate facilities for handling nuclear warheads.

The warheads themselves are designed, assembled and maintained by the Atomic Weapons Establishment (AWE) at Aldermaston and Burghfield, both in Berkshire. AWE is receiving a £1bn modernisation between 2006 and 2008, much of it to replace ageing facilities.[76] A new, powerful laser called *Orion* will replicate the conditions in a nuclear explosion. The upgrade of AWE is needed to maintain the existing UK weapons stockpile, but would clearly also be required if new weapons were to be designed and manufactured in the future.[77] As long ago as 1998, the SDR stated an intention to keep this option open.[78]

Polaris missiles were serviced at the Royal Naval Armament Depot (RNAD) Coulport, near Faslane. However, as a cost-saving measure, Britain's *Tridents* are serviced at the US facility in King's Bay, Georgia. Submarines, therefore, travel to the United States to embark missiles and return to Coulport where warheads are installed on the missiles. When going into refit, the reverse sequence is followed.

The present British government has been a good deal more open than its predecessors regarding the physical composition of the deterrent capability, including hitherto closely guarded details of stocks of nuclear materials, and detailed cost breakdowns.[79] But it has, until recently, said relatively little about associated policy matters. The retention of the deterrent is expressed as a general insurance against the future. The 2002 SDR's 'New Chapter' stated that 'the UK's nuclear weapons have a continuing use as a means of deterring major strategic military threats, and they have a continuing role in guaranteeing the ultimate security of the UK'.[80] The White Paper on the future of *Trident* published in December 2006 was somewhat more forthcoming.

CHAPTER TWO

A Nuclear Future

In 1994, as *Trident* was entering into service, Nicholas Witney, then a senior MoD official, posed the question 'whether the United Kingdom will retain the capability, and be able to muster the will, to stay in the nuclear-weapon business in the long term. Will *Trident* be the last British nuclear system?'[1] That question has become particularly pertinent because, as Clarke has pointed out more recently, 'its interests may be threatened, but as a country the UK is uniquely safe'.[2] The most fundamental issue in considering the future of the UK nuclear deterrent, therefore, is whether Britain should remain a nuclear-weapons power at all. For the first time in its nuclear history, Britain is facing that choice beyond the old Cold War, Soviet threat-dominated context. Recent government decisions notwithstanding, the question of nuclear status can be examined afresh.

Nuclear salience

A discussion of the UK's nuclear future must begin with a consideration of the role, importance and salience of nuclear weapons in what some analysts have called the second nuclear age.[3] The end of the Cold War and associated reductions in superpower arsenals initially suggested that the importance of nuclear weapons in world affairs had been significantly reduced. However, since 1998, the second nuclear age has got into its stride with the Indian and Pakistani tests of that year. Subsequently the successful review of the NPT in 2000 was followed by failure to reach international agreement at the 2005 review, and then in 2006 North Korea conducted its long-threatened nuclear test. Russia's military doctrine has placed increased emphasis on nuclear weapons to offset its conventional weakness and fading international stature.[4] China and France continue to modernise their nuclear forces, and both Britain and the United States intend to do the same. Iran looks set to become the world's tenth nuclear-weapon state. Nuclear weapons are firmly back on the international agenda. The British academic strategist Ken Booth predicts that future decades will not be characterised by 'nuclear tranquillity'.[5]

For many states, nuclear weapons are simultaneously both a problem and a solution. Uniquely threatening, they also have unique leverage because they are the most potent weapon ever devised. In Quinlan's words, 'nuclear weapons have done something unique and special to the concept of military insurance'.[6] Josiane Gabel calls them the 'capstone of military capability' because of their physical destructiveness, psychological impact and global status[7] they are 'uniquely capable of cancelling the strategic effect of all other weapons', in Colin Gray's words.[8] Moreover, when securely delivered (most obviously by ballistic missiles) they cannot themselves be cancelled by other weapons.

Gray is a persuasive, if provocative, exponent of a widely held view that nuclear weapons are here to stay: 'nuclear abolition is as hopeless of achievement as it is frequently well intentioned'.[9] No one knows how to abolish nuclear weapons[10] and they probably cannot be uninvented. Any mechanism aimed at the verification of abolition cannot be sufficiently robust as to give states full confidence in its efficacy. Britain's nuclear future is, therefore, not, or should not be, conditioned by a judgement about the desirability or feasibility of a nuclear-free world. This is not currently on offer, and is inconceivable within the first half of this century.

Gray and others argue that sooner or later nuclear use is inevitable, the Cold War experience notwithstanding.[11] Whether or not that depressing judgement is one day validated, the use or threatened use of nuclear weapons has a unique quality. Most agree that some sort of 'taboo' surrounding nuclear use has developed, though it remains to be seen how universal and dependable that taboo is. It is also difficult to devise strict a military utility for nuclear use that is not outweighed by disproportionate political consequences. The utility of nuclear weapons is largely expressed through their non-use.

The special attractiveness of nuclear weapons has been best expressed by Sir Michael Quinlan, who served as permanent secretary to the MoD between 1988 and 1992, and Colin Gray. For the former, 'a nuclear state is a state that no-one can afford to make desperate'.[12] For the latter, 'the national territory and political independence of nuclear-armed states is not to be violated or challenged, for sensible fear of the possible consequences'.[13]

The policy questions for the UK are, therefore, how to respond to a world in which nuclear weapons will continue to exist and might one day be used, and how to help to bring about a world in which nuclear weapons have reduced salience and are *not* used.

A hedge against uncertainty

During the Cold War, the rationale for the UK deterrent was easily understood, and best exemplified by the Moscow criterion and the 'second centre of decision-making'. In the absence of Cold War certainties, specific rationales for any weapon system or military capability are more difficult to devise and expound. This is perhaps most true of nuclear weapons, given that they are designed to deal with the low-likelihood/high-consequence end of the strategic spectrum associated with nuclear threats and perhaps others such as weapons of mass destruction (WMD).

Few analysts, and certainly not the British government, try to devise specific scenarios in which possession of a nuclear retaliatory capability might be the solution to the problem. This is perhaps because such predictions could become self-fulfilling if they create international tensions and resentments and if they do not, are likely to be trumped by wholly unforeseen circumstances. The current nuclear debate is looking up to 50 years ahead, a period which no one would try to predict with any confidence or credibility. This problem of predictability has been highlighted by Julian Lewis, a Conservative defence spokesman.[14] History is full of surprises, often unpleasant ones. In its recent investigation into the future of *Trident*, the House of Commons Defence Committee noted that while none of the existing nuclear-weapon powers posed an imminent military threat to the UK, 'it is not possible to predict accurately the nature of the future strategic international environment and to identify with any certainty the threats the UK is likely to face'.[15]

This uncertainty and unpredictability regarding the medium- to long-term future denies the possibility of specific scenario-based requirements for a nuclear capability. At the same time, in itself it provides the general rationale for nuclear retention: the prudent hedge against the unknowable and possibly unpleasant future. The deterrent rests, again in Quinlan's words, 'on long-term uncertainties rather than nearer-term probabilities', addressed 'to whom it may concern'.[16] John Ainslie calls this 'virtual deterrence'.[17] As Ainslie and others point out, the logic is not unique to Britain.

It provides a sound rationale for every would-be nuclear proliferator and for every other existing nuclear-weapon power.

In the absence of an unequivocal threat such as the Soviet Union, there appears to be a universal consensus that if it were not already a nuclear-weapon power, Britain would not now be seeking to become one.[18] But whatever the logical consistency, in politics giving up something you already have is not the same as not acquiring it in the first place. A decision to abandon a nuclear capability would be, after a very short time, irrevocable. This is so for two reasons. First, it would take a dramatic change in the international security scene (such as the use of a nuclear weapon somewhere) to bring about a reversal of policy. In those circumstances, the capability could not be re-created in time for it to be an adequate response to the changed situation that demanded it in the first place. Second, re-creating a nuclear-weapons infrastructure and an effective delivery system would be extremely expensive, many more times expensive than simply maintaining and, when required, updating an existing capability. In particular, having discarded *Trident*, the UK might no longer have access to an adequate delivery system. An added risk is the destabilising effect of a rush to 're-nuclearise' during crisis or war. It is, therefore, easier and politically less risky, as Ken Booth puts it, to 'do tomorrow what one did today'.[19]

In December 2006, the British government confirmed that uncertainty about the future was indeed a determining factor in deciding to extend the life of the nuclear deterrent:

> We must ... be realistic about our ability precisely to predict the nature of any future threats to our vital interests over the extended timescales associated with decisions about the renewal of our nuclear deterrent.[20]

Residual deterrence

Current official policy was spelt out in July 2006: 'we maintain the current nuclear deterrent ... because of its role in deterring acts of aggression, in insuring against the re-emergence of major strategic military threats, in preventing nuclear coercion, and in preserving peace and stability'.[21] David Broucher, former head of the UK delegation to the UN Disarmament Conference, told the Defence Committee that 'if ... there are going to be at least one, possibly two, nuclear armed countries that might be hostile to the United Kingdom, then you could make a strong case for us retaining the deterrent'.[22] This might be called the 'residual deterrence' requirement. Tony Blair himself put it this way: 'the notion of unstable, usually deeply repressive and anti-democratic states, in some cases inimical to our way of life, having a nuclear capability, is a distinct and novel reason for Britain not to give up its capacity to deter'. [23]

The identity of these potentially hostile, nuclear-armed states is more sensitive. For historical and geographical reasons, the most likely candidate must be a resurgent and bellicose Russia. Its strategic future is highly uncertain and one remaining vestige of its former superpower status is its nuclear arsenal.[24] At a greater distance, and perhaps less plausibly from a European perspective, is China. Much American strategic speculation concerns the future emergence of a new 'peer competitor' – usually China. From a British (or French, Russian, Chinese, Indian) perspective, there are already plenty of potential, nuclear-armed 'peer competitors' – each other. Such a perspective might not be relevant today, but could become so if, as Colin Gray predicts, the future includes a third nuclear age.[25] The December 2006 White Paper talks about the re-emergence of a major nuclear threat, but unsurprisingly declines to name names.[26] Clarke is unconvinced by speculative scenarios, 'none of which are worth much of the time of a policy planner, still less a politician'.[27]

Not all commentators accept this residual deterrence logic. One report from the British Pugwash Group asserts that nuclear weapons are dangerous to possess: 'at times of great international tension the weapons could attract pre-emptive strikes. Use of nuclear weapons by the UK would invite disastrous nuclear counterattack.'[28] This implies that the logic of deterrence applies to other states, but not to the UK. Quite why this should be so is not explained.

Deterrence requirements may extend beyond future animosities with other second-tier nuclear-armed powers. Potential regional adversaries continue to acquire WMD capabilities which may include nuclear weapons. On the supposition that the UK will continue to be engaged in regional 'hot-spots' including but not limited to the Middle East, military operations may have to be conducted in the face of local WMD threats. These can be posed in two ways: against deployed forces themselves (tactically) or against those forces' home country (strategically). At the very least, the unchallenged existence of local nuclear capabilities could act as a significant constraint on the UK's freedom of action and its readiness to act in support of UK interests and the wider international community.[29]

Dealing with regional 'rogues' is clearly a significant part of the rationale for continued nuclear deterrence. A cautionary note should be sounded, however. Properly and precisely targeted conventional munitions may be a more appropriate instrument, because as they are self-evidently more 'useable' they are also more credible as deterrents.[30] To date, Britain's possession of nuclear weapons has not been relevant to a series of regional crises and interventions – Suez, confrontation with Indonesia, the Falklands, and the Gulf Wars. Julian Lewis makes the point, however, that had any of the adversaries also possessed nuclear weapons, then Britain's own deterrent *would* have been very relevant.[31]

International status

It has often been alleged that no explanation of Britain's nuclear policy is complete without consideration of the international status accorded to nuclear-weapon states.[32] This was indeed the case in the early years of Britain's deterrent. But as early as 1977, Ian Smart argued that it no longer held true.[33] Possessing nuclear weapons certainly sets a country apart from the majority that do not, but whether this distinction actually constitutes status or prestige is debatable. Given its non-proliferation obligations under the NPT, no British government is today going to argue that it retains nuclear weapons for reasons of international status. That does not, of course, mean that status is not actually part of the calculus, whatever the public protestations of official policy.[34]

Quinlan argues that international status should not be a significant factor.[35] The MoD agrees – at least in public.[36] Not surprisingly, opponents of Britain's nuclear weapons also concur.[37] The coincidence between Nuclear-Weapon State (NWS) status under the NPT and permanent membership of the UN Security Council is just that – a coincidence, the latter preceding the former in all cases. Britain's standing in the world probably has more to do with its role in Europe, the Commonwealth, the UN, the G8 and many other international bodies, as well as its economic and military strength, and cultural influence. All that said, there is no getting away from the fact that nuclear weapons are special and so are the countries that own them – something clearly not lost on recent and would-be proliferators.

One aspect of Britain's nuclear status is unique – its relationship with the United States. No two other powers have such a close relationship with respect to nuclear weapons. No other nuclear power is as dependent as the UK on another state for elements of its nuclear deterrent. The Anglo-American 'special relationship' is at its most special in two areas, intelligence-sharing and nuclear cooperation, though the UK also has privileged access to conventional weapons such as *Tomahawk* cruise missiles. By virtue of the two countries' relative resources, Britain is the junior partner.

The UK's twin aims are clearly to access American nuclear resources in order to reduce its own technical and financial risk, and to seek to influence

US nuclear behaviour as the committed and sympathetic junior partner. The relationship with the United States is one of the most important and controversial aspects of the UK's nuclear policy. It is, perhaps, a moot point as to whether Britain needs the special relationship in order to maintain its nuclear capability, or whether it needs the nuclear capability in order to sustain the special relationship.

There has always been a contradiction at the heart of this relationship. The ultimate rationale for an operationally independent British nuclear capability has been the UK's unwillingness, under all conceivable circumstances, to rely on American 'extended deterrence' or a 'nuclear umbrella'.[38] This point was made by the prime minister when he described the independent deterrent as 'additional insurance against circumstances where we are threatened but America is not'.[39]

At the same time, Britain is heavily reliant upon the United States for the provision (and servicing) of its delivery system. In the past, this reliance also extended to access to a test site. There is a case that if the UK could not rely on the US nuclear guarantee of Europe, it could no longer rely on American cooperation in sustaining the British capability. This logic has led France, at much greater financial cost, to acquire a deterrent capability that is independent in acquisition, as well as independent in operational control.[40] Britain has chosen to stress independence of use in order to maintain its deterrent at significantly lower cost.

It is a subject for intense debate as to whether this relationship gives the UK useful influence with the United States, or whether it has led to an unhealthy dependence and the standing of 'loyal vassal'.[41] Clare Short, a former Labour cabinet minister, argues that 'replacing Trident will tie UK foreign policy to US policy for decades to come. It would prevent the UK from acting with others on global warming, poverty and conflict, and perpetuate our role as US poodle.'[42] Rodric Braithwaite, a former chairman of the UK government's Joint Intelligence Committee, believes 'a deterrent dependent on the US is an undesirable constraint on our freedom of action'.[43] Greenpeace goes further in asserting that the only way Britain's *Trident* could be used would be to legitimise a US pre-emptive strike.[44]

Britain's ties with the United States are its most important relationship with another single country. The effect on that relationship of the UK's decision to retain, or relinquish, its nuclear weapons could be significant. The symbology of nuclear weapons is important. It may be that a decision to give up nuclear weapons would be taken as a sign of a changed role for Britain in the world, in which it might no longer be prepared to act as the chief ally of the United States. Alternatively, if Britain were to remain a close and useful ally in all other respects, the result of relinquishing nuclear weapons might be modest. Much depends on the question posed earlier – is the nuclear alliance a foundation of the Anglo-American relationship, or a consequence of it?[45] Caroline Lucas, a Green Party MEP, argues that with no clear military threat and a positive relationship with the world's only superpower, if Britain cannot give up its nuclear weapons now, it never will.[46]

The response of the United States is not the decisive factor in Britain's decision about its future nuclear status, nor should it be. Attitudes towards Britain's nuclear relationship with the US – trusted partner or compliant subordinate – depend on wider views about both nuclear weapons and the United States. But Britain's nuclear stance is inseparable from the wider ramifications of the special relationship. There will always be an instinct in official and political circles not to 'rock the boat'. In June 2004, the 1958 Agreement was extended again for a further ten years. President George W. Bush judged that 'it is in our [US] interest to continue to assist them [the UK] in maintaining a credible nuclear force'.[47]

Another friendly country features in British thinking on nuclear weapons – France. Though official policy never acknowledges this, it seems that a British government would be reluctant to yield to France the status of the European Union's sole nuclear-weapon state.[48] Would, indeed, the rest of Europe wish to see France with a nuclear monopoly on the continent? Perhaps more substantively, as long ago as 1967 Edward Heath spoke of British nuclear weapons being held 'in trust' for Europe.[49] This can be seen as part of the balancing of the transatlantic partnership, or as a hedge against future US disengagement from Europe[50] – and the two positions are by no means mutually exclusive.

Recent years have seen increased Anglo-French cooperation on nuclear matters. In November 1992 the two countries established the Franco-British Joint Commission on Nuclear Policy and Doctrine, whose low-key consultations have continued since then. In 2003 the French president and British prime minister reiterated an earlier statement that 'we do not see situations arising in which the vital interest of either France or the United Kingdom could be threatened without the vital interests of the other also being threatened'.[51] Furthermore, it is clear from their respective public statements that the two governments have near-identical conceptions of nuclear deterrence.[52] Perhaps the greatest difference between the two countries is that in France there is no significant debate about the country's nuclear status. If there were to be just one nuclear power in Western Europe, it would be France.

Domestic politics

Britain's nuclear policy enjoys broad cross-party support. This has not always been the case. While the Conservative Party has always advocated retention of the nuclear deterrent, Labour has only done so consistently when in government. In opposition, Labour has flirted with, and sometimes made party policy, unilateral nuclear disarmament. This was the case most notably in the 1980s, when Labour was not in power. A significant part of the Labour Party remains opposed to all things nuclear – civil as well as military.

It is now received wisdom that for fear of another long period out of office, Labour's present leadership will not contemplate abandoning the deterrent in any circumstances short of universal nuclear disarmament. On coming to power in 1997, abolition of the nuclear deterrent was the one subject specifically ruled out of discussion in the SDR.[53] Today, having retained *Trident* for almost a decade while in power, it would take a very marked change in policy, prompted by an equally dramatic external event or internal re-consideration, to make a Labour government decide to give the deterrent up. Before the 2005 general election, Tony Blair stated that 'we've got to retain our nuclear deterrent ... we've had an independent nuclear deterrent for a long time. Now that decision is for another time, but in principle, I believe it's important to retain our own ... independent deterrent.'[54] This position was reiterated in Parliament on 22 November 2006.[55]

The nuclear issue remains divisive within the Labour Party. But the party leadership remains committed to the nuclear deterrent, despite a view that 'Labour is set to enjoy the unique distinction of having held two diametrically opposed positions on nuclear weapons within the space of 20 years – and being equally wrong on both occasions'.[56] The Conservative position is also clear: 'we will retain, and when the time comes, update our nuclear deterrent'.[57] Even within the Conservative Party, however, there are dissident voices. A former defence secretary, Michael Portillo, has argued publicly in favour of unilateral nuclear disarmament.[58] It may be that just as only Labour could reform the welfare system, or Richard Nixon could establish relations with communist China, so only the Conservatives could give up the nuclear deterrent. At the moment, however, that remains a distant prospect.

During the Cold War public opinion polls consistently showed a significant popular majority in favour of the independent nuclear deterrent. Today public opinion is more evenly split, as demonstrated in a MORI poll in October 2005, and again in December 2006 in a poll conducted by Populus for *The Times*.[59] The disappearance of the old Soviet threat makes this unsurprising, though events such as the North Korean test keep the spectre of nuclear threats alive. The strategic rationale for continuing with the deterrent may be vague, but the political imperative is very clear.

Legality

Much of the public debate over nuclear weapons is conducted in terms of their legality. The issues relate primarily to the NPT, under which the UK is one of five recognised NWS. There have also been recent legal opinions delivered on the legality of the possession, threat and actual use of nuclear weapons.[60] The nature of the legal arguments is such that proponents and opponents of nuclear deterrence alike can find support for their respective cases.[61]

A basic observation is worth making. International treaties, from which most international law derives, are diplomatic as much as legal instruments. To advance arguments, on either side of a case, in purely legal terms is, therefore, to ignore the political context of those agreements, which over time may become progressively less relevant to contemporary circumstances. This was certainly true, for example, of the 1972 ABM Treaty, devised in a very different era from the one in which it was finally abrogated by the United States 30 years later.[62]

Article VI of the NPT commits the five NWS to the eventual elimination of nuclear weapons, in what is sometimes described as a 'grand bargain'[63] with the non-nuclear states. Lucas accuses Britain, and by implication the other NWS, of negotiating in bad faith.[64] From the other side of the debate, Gray agrees.[65]

The commitment to total nuclear disarmament is perhaps most usefully viewed as a long-term aspiration rather than an immediate legal obligation. The NPT does not ban nuclear weapons outright, in the way that chemical and biological weapons are prohibited by other treaties.[66] It also sets the elimination of nuclear weapons alongside 'a Treaty on general and complete disarmament', a target which is not remotely in sight and perhaps best illustrates the aspirational nature of the commitment to eventual nuclear abolition.[67] In terms of the current debate about Britain's nuclear future, the NPT certainly does not require any unilateral abandonment of nuclear weapons.

The importance of a decision to retain or abandon nuclear weapons is such that no British government will determine its policy on the basis of the equivocal, open-ended diplomatic undertakings of 1968. It will, however, ensure that its stance is fully justifiable in terms of those undertakings and will make whatever gestures, substantive or not, that it judges possible in the broad direction of the NPT's aspirations. The government has made its own position clear: 'renewing our minimum nuclear deterrent capability is fully consistent with all our international obligations'.[68]

The non-proliferation regime embodied in the NPT is often cited as an area where Britain could set a positive example, as well as living up to what some believe to be its legal obligations under the treaty. The corollary is that a decision to renew or replace *Trident* sets a poor example, and encourages other states to acquire their own nuclear weapons. One commentator says that 'others have been listening and they have been learning the lesson we've been teaching'.[69] The British American Security Information Council suggests that:

> Replacing Trident would send a clear message to aspirant nuclear powers that the UK continues to attach strategic and political importance to nuclear weapons. It would not only legitimise nuclear weapon possession but it would encourage states with far greater and immediate strategic threats to their vital interests and territorial integrity than the UK to go down the nuclear route.[70]

Conversely, 'if Trident were not replaced then Britain would be making a positive contribution to tackling proliferation. We would be saying to other states that nuclear weapons are not a suitable response to specific or general concerns.'[71] A British decision to abandon nuclear weapons could well be seen in this light. But this approach can be very patronising. Other governments do not need Britain to 'set them an example'. They will continue to make their own decisions according to their own perceptions of their security needs and the resources available. It cannot be demonstrated that other states would follow, or even be significantly influenced by, a British decision to abandon nuclear weapons It may be attractive for Britain to seize the moral high ground and deny other countries the opportunity to accuse the UK of hypocrisy when it seeks to prevent states such as Iran securing what it already has itself. But public displays of moral virtue are a poor basis for policy-making.

It is true that a necessarily public decision to extend or replace *Trident* will indicate that Britain intends to remain a nuclear power for many years to come, and that it sees no prospect of the NPT Article VI aspirations becoming a reality. This could be seen either as a cynical betrayal of the UK's non-proliferation obligations or as a sensible recognition of strategic realities.

To be fair to those who press for unilateral nuclear disarmament, very few of them argue that Britain could set off a 'domino effect' whereby other countries might be inspired to follow the UK's example. There is no serious prospect of any of the other four NWS following such a UK lead and nor would recent or aspirant proliferators such as Pakistan or Iran have their own strategic calculations reversed by Britain's actions. By leaving the nuclear 'club' the UK might be better placed diplomatically to lead future non-proliferation efforts,[72] but the case for abandonment cannot with honesty be put any more strongly.

Cost[73]

No decision about Britain's nuclear future can be taken without reference to the financial cost entailed, both in terms of absolute cost and its opportunity cost. Hugely speculative and sometimes arbitrary figures have been quoted for replacing *Trident*, broadly in the range of £10bn[74] to £75bn.[75] The government estimates a total cost in the range of £15–20bn representing the price of four new submarines[76] and some refurbishment of missiles, warheads and infrastructure. Spread over about 15 years, this represents about £1bn per annum on average.

Though this is, in absolute terms, a significant sum, in relation not only to the importance of the issue, but also to UK government spending currently running at more than £500bn per year, the additional amount that might be spent on *Trident* appears trivial. In relation to defence spending it is much more significant, and this is where a significant opportunity cost arises. This may explain why the political role of nuclear weapons is stressed – in order to attract Treasury funding from outside the existing, already pressured, defence budget.[77]

A nuclear future

There are plenty of voices asserting that Britain should give up its nuclear weapons. The British Pugwash Group, for example, argues that 'the benefits to Britain of maintaining its nuclear arsenal are hard to discern and the arguments in favour of so doing can be shown to be specious and misguided'.[78] Michael MccGwire believes that getting rid of the nuclear deterrent would reap benefits in terms of non-proliferation, greater autonomy from the United States and enhanced conventional forces.[79] For others, nuclear weapons are illegal and immoral.[80] Some question the relevance of nuclear weapons to today's security threats.[81] Even NATO states that 'in the current international strategic environment, Allies have declared that the circumstances in which they might have to contemplate any use of nuclear weapons are extremely remote'.[82]

Nonetheless, Britain continues to regard nuclear weapons as a regrettable necessity, distasteful but also prudent.[83] The 1998 SDR's assessment endures today: 'while large nuclear arsenals and risks of proliferation remain our minimum deterrent remains a necessary element of security'.[84] The long-term strategic advantage of a prudent hedge against an unpredictable future outweighs the more immediate and modest costs, financial and diplomatic. The British government's December 2006 White Paper makes it very clear that the UK is to retain its nuclear weapons.

In 1977, in relation to the replacement of *Polaris*, Smart identified the key questions that remain pertinent today:

> it is ... that implicit role as a 'last resort' national deterrent which constitutes, in the final analysis, the only fully rational argument for the present British deterrent's existence...

Who, however, is to be deterred, from what kind of aggression, and by what type of threat?

> Is it ... only an unprovoked attack on the United Kingdom itself which is at issue, or is it also attacks upon British allies or British external interests? Is it only a nuclear attack which is to be deterred...?[85]

In sum, how should the British deterrent function?

CHAPTER THREE

Nuclear Deterrence

Possessing a 'nuclear deterrent' is not the same as engaging in 'deterrence' or, when required, actually 'deterring' someone else. The 'deterrent' is the instrument by which a policy of deterrence is executed. It need not be a nuclear instrument. The act of deterrence, whether successful or not, is as old as human society.[1] A key aspect of nuclear deterrence is also ancient, and pre-dates the invention of nuclear weapons themselves. It is 'hostage-taking' on a truly grand scale, entailing the explicit threat to 'execute' thousands of the enemy's civilian population – but in contrast to historical practice they don't first have to be taken captive physically.[2]

The British concept of deterrence is simple: 'inducing someone to refrain from unwanted action by putting before him the prospect that taking it will prompt a response with disadvantages to him outweighing the advantages of the action'.[3] To deter is to frighten.[4]

Two points should be stressed. First, deterrence seeks to maintain the status quo, because it aims to *prevent* action by another party (in contrast to *coercion* which tries to force the other party *to* act).[5] Secondly, the key decision-maker is the other party, who decides whether or not to be deterred. Deploying a supposed 'deterrent' by no means ensures that others will be 'deterred'.

In order to deter another party from taking action seen as undesirable, three conditions must be met. The deterring party must have the physical capability to impose the required costs on the 'deterree', and must have the will to use that capability. In addition, and most importantly, the deterring party must be able to communicate effectively with the deterree.[6] Indeed, effective communication can, to some degree, compensate for a lack of will and/or capability through a process of bluffing. Without the ability to communicate, however, the would-be deterring party's capability and will cannot deter, as the putative deterree will not get the message.

Because the aim of deterrence is to prevent something from happening, there is usually no evidence for its success. It can rarely be proved, and then only after the event, that the act of deterrence actually altered behaviour. After all, nothing happened. It is possible that the deterree didn't even know he was being deterred, if the undesirable course of action was not even being contemplated, or was decided against for reasons unconnected with the threats, understood or not, made by the deterring party. By contrast, when deterrence fails it is immediately obvious, as the undesirable action does take place.[7]

It was during the nuclear age that deterrence assumed a dominant position in strategic discourse. The consequences of even limited use of nuclear weapons made standards of worthwhile defence impossibly high. The only alternative was to prevent nuclear use in the first place, and in the adversarial context of the Cold War only deterrence would suffice. Deterrence in the nuclear age acquired a body of thought almost amounting to a theology, though Lawrence Freedman judges that deterrence worked better in practice than in theory.[8] None of the theory was fully tested except in the obvious sense that whether Cold War nuclear deterrence worked or not, it self-evidently did not fail.[9]

Some aspects of nuclear deterrence are perennial – the physical workings of nuclear weapons and their effects, and the essential nature and requirements of deterrence. But the context within which each works has changed beyond recognition. Whatever its role today and in the future, nuclear deterrence no longer occupies centre-stage in international relations in the way that it did during the bipolar superpower stand-off of the Cold War.

Today's nuclear world is much more diffuse. A single superpower – the United States – retains an abundance of nuclear weapons and delivery systems. Among the second-tier powers most are also nuclear armed (Britain, France, Russia, China and India). Others are not, but could become so (Japan and, less plausibly, Germany). Some strictly regional powers have nuclear weapons (Israel, Pakistan and North Korea). At least one other country (Iran) looks set to become a nuclear power. Others might decide to acquire nuclear weapons if their security prospects seemed to warrant it (South Korea, Taiwan, Saudi Arabia and Egypt, to name just a few speculative possibilities). Often overlooked are the 'quasi-nuclear powers', a hangover from the Cold War. Six NATO countries have forces trained and equipped to deliver US nuclear weapons – Germany, the Netherlands, Belgium, Italy, Greece and Turkey. Finally, numerous allies of the US are protected by the 'extended deterrence' provided by the United States – all NATO member states practice a policy of nuclear deterrence through the Alliance.

This context prompts the essential questions – who is going to deter whom, and how are they going to do it? How much of our existing understanding of nuclear deterrence is relevant to the second nuclear age, or even to a future third nuclear age? Keith Payne observes that:

> compared to the Cold War era, the list of provocations and opponents we now hope to deter has expanded, the contexts within which we hope to deter are far more variable, as are the stakes involved and the priority we may attach to deterrence ... much of our Cold War-derived thinking about deterrence now needs to be reconsidered.[10]

The 'one-size-fits-all' approach will not work.[11]

Deterring what?

It is clear that the principal task of nuclear weapons is to deter the use of other nuclear weapons. Some argue that this is, or should be, their sole function.[12] The use of a nuclear weapon would have greater and more immediate adverse consequences than any other man-made event, and the prevention of a nuclear attack is sufficiently important on its own to warrant the scale of the UK's deterrent effort. The utility of nuclear weapons is in their 'non-use'.[13] If nuclear weapons can only ever be used to respond to other nuclear use, they cannot be used in the first place.

Others suggest that nuclear weapons have a wider utility.[14] It is also argued that nuclear weapons alone cannot deter, and that a broader spectrum of responses, not all military, is needed to address the diverse circumstances in which a state might want to dissuade another from taking certain actions including, but not only, nuclear attack.[15] The current US administration agrees: 'deterrence can no longer be based solely on the threat of nuclear retaliation'.[16] The 1998 SDR made the interesting and important point that possession of a nuclear deterrent can prevent nuclear coercion.[17] In other words, nuclear threats against a non-nuclear state can be used to force, as well as to prevent, certain actions. The possession of one's own nuclear capability cancels out this threat of 'blackmail' – nuclear blackmail being a nuclear deterrent in the wrong hands.[18]

What other threats might nuclear weapons be used to deter? Some broad possibilities exist: the use of other WMD by states, nuclear or other WMD-armed terrorism, and the initiation of war itself.

WMD use by states

The term 'WMD' conceals a profound disparity of effect between nuclear weapons on the one hand, and chemical and biological weapons (CBW) on the other. The contemporary term 'CBRN' (chemical, biological, radiological, nuclear) is more inclusive, but similarly obscures the distinctive nature of nuclear weapons. All WMD have severe consequences in terms of human casualties and physical contamination. But only nuclear weapons have extensive blast and heat effects. Their impact is much more immediate and they cause unparalleled physical destruction. Large-scale 'weaponisation' and effective delivery of CBW and radiological devices pose severe threats, but these types of WMD do not pose a threat on the scale and severity of nuclear weapons.[19]

The question of a nuclear response to non-nuclear WMD is an important issue because the UK, in common with most other states,[20] has eschewed the possession of CBW. Britain cannot respond, or threaten to respond, to CBW use in kind. Though unhelpful in some respects, the grouping of all CBRN weapons under the WMD label at least leaves open the deterrent suggestion that *any* WMD use might be met with the *only* WMD response available to the UK – nuclear weapons. But a nuclear response to the use of other WMD (or threatened response in the case of a deterrence posture) could be viewed as disproportionate and thus lacking in credibility.

An alternative to 'going nuclear' in response to CBW attack is the use of advanced, precision conventional weapons and effective passive defences.[21] This would be the preferred, if not always adequate, approach to deterring such attacks. Explicitly ruling out a 'limited' nuclear response to anything short of a nuclear attack has its drawbacks, however. If a nuclear response to CBW use is definitely *not* on the cards, one inhibition has certainly been removed. On the other hand, if a nuclear bluff is called and a nuclear response does not follow CBW aggression, overall deterrence may be seriously undermined.[22]

During the first Gulf War in 1991, US official statements at least implied that if Saddam Hussein used chemical weapons, he might face a nuclear response. It was later announced that the United States would *not* have used nuclear weapons but nonetheless the expectation that it might appears to have had the desired deterrent effect.[23] The Iraqi regime did accept its expulsion from Kuwait without resorting to chemical weapons which it previously *had* been prepared to use against domestic opponents. Because the implied threat is now known to have been a bluff, the efficacy of this tactic in the future must now be compromised. The credibility of a nuclear threat in response to CBW use is further undermined by the likely disproportionate cost in civilian casualties.[24]

The UK's declared stance is ambivalent. A junior defence minister said in 1998 that 'the use of chemical or biological weapons by any state would be a grave breach of international law. A state which chose to use chemical or biological weapons against the UK should expect us to exercise our right of self-defence and to make a proportionate response.'[25] More recent statements have been equally ambiguous, but have not ruled out a nuclear response to CBW use explicitly,[26] despite the Negative Security Assurance (NSA) towards non-nuclear states. On another occasion, however, a nuclear response to Iraqi CBW use was ruled out explicitly and, by implication, to *any* CBW use.[27]

Though CBRN proliferation is mentioned in general terms, the 2006 White Paper contains no explicit reference to nuclear deterrence in relation to other WMD. This is perhaps not surprising, not least because of legal and proportionality implications.[28] Nor would the government wish specifically to rule out such action, for fear of encouraging CBW proliferation and use. An explicit threat might be appropriate in a particular crisis where the scale and consequences of CBW or radiological use may make a limited nuclear response proportionate and credible.

WMD-armed terrorism

In October 2005 Blair stated: 'I do not think that anyone pretends that the independent nuclear deterrent is a defence against terrorism.'[29] Intuitively, that must be true. But in the face of Western (particularly American) conventional military superiority, putative opponents can adopt one of two strategies – to 'trade up' to WMD, or to 'trade down' to terrorism and insurgency. It is when those two approaches are combined in WMD terrorism that nuclear deterrence might have some relevance.[30]

Nuclear terrorism could take several forms – the theft and detonation of a complete weapon (probably not from a Western nuclear state), construction of a 'home-made' improvised nuclear device, or sabotage of a nuclear facility (such as a civil power station).[31] Terrorist use of other WMD is also possible, some even argue likely, though the caveats noted above in respect of nuclear deterrence to counter non-nuclear WMD still apply in the terrorist case.

A nuclear response (and, therefore, the credibility of a deterrent stance) to nuclear terrorism poses several fundamental problems. First is the difficulty in establishing responsibility for the attack, unless it is self-proclaimed. A nuclear response after a lengthy criminal and forensic investigation to identify the perpetrators is neither appropriate nor credible. Second is the absence of a 'return address' in terms of suitable targets. Terrorist networks lack the identifiable, physical infrastructure of a state. Thirdly, a nuclear response possibly entailing mass civilian casualties unconnected with the terrorist group responsible is self-evidently disproportionate. A further inhibition to nuclear retaliation is that apocalyptic terrorist groups such as al-Qaeda might actually welcome nuclear escalation.[32]

Terrorist groups, however, are not entirely non-territorial, divorced from any sovereign government or state. This was demonstrated by al-Qaeda's relationship with Afghanistan's Taliban government prior to the 11 September 2001 attacks. In that instance, the unequivocal linkage between the (non-nuclear) atrocities in the United States and an identifiable state government warranted large-scale (non-nuclear) action against the Taliban. Large-scale terrorism involving the acquisition and delivery of WMD, particularly a nuclear device, would require some form of sanctuary and sophisticated facilities. Terrorism cannot emanate from a territorial void.

This observation leads to the conclusion that WMD-armed terrorists are likely to be either state sanctioned or state surrogates.[33] That is, they either act with the connivance of a state government which lends at least passive support, or are themselves an 'irregular' and possibly anonymous agent *of* a state. The extent to which such groups warrant a different set of responses from their state sponsors, therefore, depends on the nature of their relationship and the extent to which it is verifiable. Suicidal, apocalyptic terrorists may not themselves be deterrable, but their state allies probably are. Gray has observed that 'terrorists require support, and, *to the degree that they require state support*, the states that support them are capable of being deterred' [emphasis added].[34] Tertrais told the House of Commons Defence Committee that where there was 'incontrovertible evidence' of state sponsorship of WMD terrorism, we enter the realm of vital interests where there can be a role for nuclear deterrence.[35]

The risks inherent in provoking a nuclear-armed state are likely to act as a significant deterrent to identifiable state sponsorship of nuclear terrorism. Canadian analyst Robin Frost points out that no government with access to nuclear-weapons technology is likely to hand its 'national treasures' over to groups outside its direct control.[36] If the groups *are* under direct control, they remain agents of that state like any other delivery system. Wherever identifiable links exist between states and WMD-armed terrorists, deterrence remains relevant. In contrast to Blair's remark of October 2005 cited above, in December 2006 the government explicitly threatened a nuclear response to state-sponsored nuclear terrorism.[37]

General war-prevention

A role for nuclear weapons in general war-prevention has long been part of NATO strategy. During the Cold War, the West's nuclear weapons were used to offset the Warsaw Pact's substantial numerical advantage in conventional arms, especially on the Central Front in Europe. The Alliance always retained the option of resorting to a nuclear response if conventional forces were overwhelmed by a Soviet attack. NATO's readiness to escalate to nuclear use was a major part of its overall deterrence strategy.[38]

General war-prevention remains formally part of NATO's doctrine: 'the fundamental purpose of the nuclear forces of the Allies is political: to preserve peace and prevent coercion *and any kind of war*'[39] [emphasis added]. However, despite this formal declaration the circumstances under which NATO could not now respond adequately to aggression by using its conventional forces alone are difficult to envisage. Instead, the option of escalating to nuclear use now seems to lie with potential adversaries needing to offset NATO's post-Cold War conventional superiority.[40]

Nonetheless, the danger of escalation to nuclear war remains a powerful deterrent to major war between nuclear-armed states. In 1981, Kenneth Waltz wrote that '[nuclear] deterrent strategies induce caution all round and thus reduce the incidence of war ... war between nuclear-armed nation-states will be unlikely to start'.[41] He made this point while arguing that nuclear proliferation was not necessarily a bad thing. This approach can be summed up in the idea that 'a nuclear neighbourhood is a polite neighbourhood'. One need not actually favour nuclear proliferation to recognise that a potential adversary's possession of nuclear weapons will usually cause policy-makers to exercise substantial restraint – but only where nuclear weapons are perceived to be useable. Nuclear weapons will inhibit the start of major wars that might threaten national survival and so lead to nuclear escalation. They will not deter lesser adventurism where the use of nuclear weapons would be disproportionate and so not credible as a deterrent – for example, the 1982 Falklands War.

In today's circumstances it is difficult to incorporate general war-prevention into a deterrence doctrine, not least because of problems of proportionality and establishing escalation mechanisms outside a Cold-

War context. However, it remains the case that the presence of nuclear weapons will have the effect of making major war less likely between nuclear-armed states.

The workings of deterrence

The general caution induced by the 'fearsomeness'[42] of nuclear weapons is known as 'existential' deterrence. Britain's nuclear stance has always contained an element of existentialism – the 'ultimate guarantee' of security provided by the deterrent effect of merely possessing nuclear weapons.[43] This is especially so with the demise of the target-specific Moscow criterion and its replacement by the 'To Whom It May Concern' nature of current policy.[44] Existential deterrence means that nuclear weapons deter simply by their very nature, irrespective of the specifics of particular nuclear strategies.[45] Nuclear weapons deter because once nuclear-armed states go to war with each other, no-one knows where it will lead.[46]

Discussion of how nuclear weapons might actually be used can be taken to imply that they have become weapons for warfighting rather than war-prevention. However, as Quinlan puts it, 'weapons deter by the possibility of their use, and by no other route; the distinction sometimes attempted between deterrent capabilities and war-fighting capabilities has ... no meaningful basis'.[47] Nuclear weapons – the deterrent – are the instrument of deterrence, not its actuality. The party one wishes to deter must be persuaded that one might be prepared to use that instrument, otherwise the deterrent will not deter. Payne calls existential deterrence 'a dangerous myth'.[48] This may be an exaggeration because of the 'cautionary' effect of nuclear weapons, but clearly possession alone is not sufficient as a deterrent. Gray advises that 'a nuclear power must devise strategic guidance for its nuclear armament'.[49] Even if one does not wish to fight a nuclear war, deterrence credibility requires that one can threaten it: 'the evident possession of practical options is directed entirely to making war as remote an eventuality as possible'.[50] If, on the other hand, one relies largely on the existential awfulness of nuclear weapons for their deterrent effect, the party most likely to be deterred will be oneself. A nuclear stance that is self-deterring is unlikely to deter anyone else.

A deterrence stance must be credible not just to the deterree, but also to the deterring party. In crises short of those threatening national survival, there are powerful disincentives for nuclear use. Any such use, however 'limited' and accurately targeted, carries a near-certainty of widespread non-combatant casualties. The conditions under which a nuclear response might be appropriate and proportionate are, therefore, strictly limited. General Lee Butler, a former commander-in-chief of US Strategic Command, asks 'What target would warrant such retaliation? Would we hold an entire society accountable for the decision of a single demented leader?'[51] One does not have to agree with Butler's abolitionist answer to recognise the validity of his question. Persuading others that under certain circumstances we *would* contemplate using nuclear weapons is much the same issue as persuading *ourselves* that we would.[52]

The problem that proportionality poses for effective deterrence lies behind the development of 'useable', low-yield weapons, of which *Trident*'s sub-strategic configuration is one example. The credibility of a weapon's use may be inversely proportional to its yield, making higher-yield Cold War-legacy weapons of diminishing utility for second-nuclear-age deterrence. Payne puts it this way: 'the credibility of the US [and, by implication, the UK] nuclear deterrent may rest not on how much damage to the opponent's society is threatened, but rather on how little'.[53]

A debate about the war-fighting role of nuclear weapons was initiated by the United States' 2001 Nuclear Posture Review (NPR).[54] The NPR replaced the old 'strategic triad' of intercontinental ballistic missiles (ICBMs), SLBMs and manned bombers (all nuclear systems), with a 'new triad' comprising offensive systems (both nuclear and conventional), defences (such as BMD) and a 'responsive infrastructure' (the ability to reconfigure forces to meet emerging threats). This suggests a reduced reliance on nuclear weapons for strategic deterrence, and the NPR also notes that new precision-guided conventional weapons can accomplish some existing nuclear missions. But the NPR also states that nuclear weapons could be used to attack certain targets such as deeply buried bunkers which are resistant to conventional attack, of which it says there are 1,400 worldwide.

It has been claimed that this new triad lowers the nuclear threshold and makes nuclear weapons more 'useable'.[55] Others believe that more useable weapons allow for the targeting of high-value assets with reduced collateral damage, thereby enhancing deterrence credibility.[56] A more 'useable' weapon is, therefore, less likely to be used. Gray makes the point that:

> In the new environment, we are not in the business of having nuclear threats to destroy populations. If we ever had to use those weapons, they should be employed against very particular targets for very particular purposes, and that requires a nuclear arsenal that is not really the nuclear arsenal we have which we have inherited from the Cold War.[57]

For the UK, the position should be clear. 'Useable' nuclear weapons pose a more credible threat and thereby strengthen deterrence, not substitute for it.

If deterrence should fail, a further dilemma arises. Should one retaliate, the threat of which failed to deter in the first place? To what end? Revenge is no basis for sound strategy. But it may be necessary to re-establish the deterrence credibility that clearly had been lost, but which, short of an all-out nuclear exchange, will still be relevant. Moreover, a determination to retaliate is essential in ensuring that one is not self-deterred in the first place, or that one's determination is not doubted by parties which need to be deterred.

During the Cold War, the West's deterrence relationship with the Soviet Union essentially involved a symmetrical balance between two huge and broadly similar arsenals, even if the Soviet view of deterrence was not the same as NATO's. In the second nuclear age, that symmetry has gone, though it might re-emerge in a putative future third nuclear age. For Western countries at least, national survival currently appears not to be at stake, barring the unlikely scenario of a cataclysmic breakdown in relations with Russia. Instead, security threats come from highly asymmetrical regional adversaries.

Britain's Cold-War deterrence posture amounted to the deterrence of the strong by the relatively weak. Targeting Moscow and other key aspects of Soviet power provided the key leverage that allowed a much smaller and less powerful state to achieve adequate deterrence of a superpower opponent. Today, no such requirement exists. Britain's most likely deterrence need is in relation to relatively weak opponents. Potential regional opponents may use WMD to deter Western intervention and to offset Western conventional superiority. Importantly for deterrence, the 'asymmetrical' nature of potential conflicts extends beyond different means, but also to ends.[58] Regional opponents may have a great deal more at stake (including regime survival) than the US and its allies, even if Western 'vital interests', however defined, are involved. This was clearly the case in Vietnam and, more recently, Iraq.

The stakes at hand will determine the resolve and tolerance of pain of the respective adversaries.[59] Added to that is an asymmetry of scruples. Future adversaries may be willing both to inflict and to suffer consequences that Western governments and populations are not. The former Serbian president Slobodan Milosevic stated that 'I am ready to walk on corpses, and the West is not. That is why I shall win.'[60] He was wrong about winning, but right about his regime's ruthlessness. Western governments may have greater regard for authoritarian states' civilian populations than do their own rulers.[61] Devising a credible deterrence posture for an opponent who is more cost and risk tolerant will always be difficult. As Freedman observes, 'the asymmetry in capabilities goes in one direction; the asymmetry in interests goes in another'.[62] The result is a highly asymmetrical conflict in which the interests at stake may be more important than the tools to hand. This is exacerbated by a potential lack of mutual comprehension. Understanding different value-sets and modes of thinking is essential for successful, opponent-oriented deterrence postures. One does not have to believe that Third World dictators are irrational or undeterrable to recognise that Western understanding of their priorities and decision-making processes may be imperfect. So too, may be their understanding of the West's.[63]

One feature of Cold-War deterrence does endure. Deterrence can be, though it is not always, a two-way process. Others will seek to deter us as we seek to deter them. Potential opponents may use their WMD capabilities to dissuade us from intervening in matters of 'vital interest' to them. Alternatively, they may seek to offset our capabilities – 'deterring the deterrent'[64] in order to 'level the playing-field'. Western countries in turn, of course, will want to deter *their* deterrents.

Robert O'Neill suggests that the possession of nuclear weapons was previously limited to the 'top dogs', but that they are now becoming the weapons of the 'underdogs'.[65] Britain's possession of nuclear weapons during the Cold War was of the 'underdog' type despite the early view that nuclear weapons restored the UK's Great Power status. A threat by the underdog to use nuclear weapons against a stronger opponent might lack credibility, as the UK understood all too well, but may be necessary for national (or regime) survival. North Korea has demonstrated how a nuclear capability (even an embryonic one) can be used to gain substantial leverage against a much stronger, more risk-averse, opponent.[66] It could be argued that Iraq, the one member of Bush's 'Axis of Evil' to be attacked, was the one with the least-developed nuclear programme. At the very least, the presence of local WMD capabilities may complicate Western policy-making.[67]

As Gray asserts, 'for states desperate to discourage intervention in their locality by an interfering sheriff protecting western notions of international order, nuclear status is the best-looking answer to the local strategist's prayer'.[68]

Nuclear weapons provide a shield behind which local disputes can be resolved and local adventures undertaken. Colonel Muammar Gadhafi of

Libya put it graphically: 'if we had possessed a deterrent – missiles that could reach New York – we would have hit it at the same moment [as US air strikes]. Consequently, we should build this force so that they and others will no longer think about an attack.'[69] The conclusion to be drawn from this brief look at others' proliferation and deterrence motivations is that the UK could be deterred as much as it might seek to deter others itself. The mutual nature of this relationship in certain scenarios needs to be fully recognised in devising Britain's own nuclear-deterrence requirements and strategy. Deterrence does not work in a vacuum.

Nuclear declarations

With the sole and important exception of the loosely defined Moscow criterion, Britain has adopted a policy of 'studied ambiguity' regarding the potential employment of its nuclear weapons. The official stance was spelt out as recently as December 2006:

> We deliberately maintain ambiguity about precisely when, how and at what scale we would contemplate use of our nuclear deterrent. We will not simplify the calculations of a potential aggressor by defining more precisely the circumstances in which we might consider the use of our nuclear capabilities.[70]

This is fully in line with NATO strategy: 'they [nuclear weapons] will continue to fulfil an essential role by ensuring uncertainty in the mind of any aggressor about the nature of the Allies' response to military aggression'.[71] Thomas Schelling's 'threat that leaves something to chance'[72] makes sense in that it avoids making public commitments in advance ('lines in the sand'), which, if honoured, might be inappropriate in the circumstances or if ignored would undermine future deterrence credibility. It is also undesirable explicitly to rule out certain options in order not to encourage just those courses of action. It is only necessary to communicate both power and resolve to resist objectionable acts.[73] The 'To Whom it May Concern' nature of current deterrence requirements probably makes this approach inevitable. In the absence of an identifiable deterree, a policy of ambiguity may simply be a recognition that it is impossible to be more specific or, within an alliance context, that a degree of vagueness is necessary to maintain cohesion. The danger, of course, is that ambiguity about one's likely response can lead to a bluff being called, or one's genuine deterrent threat being questioned. Studied ambiguity and effective communication may be at odds just when a credible threat of retaliation is most needed. Deterrence can be weakened, or even fail altogether, if there is uncertainty (or a misreading of intentions) as to whether a forceful response will be forthcoming.

Closely related to ambiguity is the issue of 'no first use'. UK policy is unequivocal, but ambiguous: 'we will not rule in or out the first use of nuclear weapons'.[74] The debate as to whether states should make formal declarations that they will not be the first to use nuclear weapons has a long pedigree. Proponents of such a policy argue that it makes clear that the role of nuclear weapons is simply to deter nuclear attack and that the state concerned will itself never initiate nuclear use.[75] It is argued that other than nuclear attack, every form of aggression can be countered, and so deterred, by advanced conventional means. However, conventional deterrence has proved much less reliable than nuclear deterrence[76] and, as Malcolm Rifkind said in 1994, 'a no-first-use declaration would take us out of the realm of war prevention and into the realm of war limitation'.[77] This is not, as sometimes alleged,[78] a policy of nuclear first use but an unwillingness to indicate that non-nuclear (but possibly other WMD) aggression can proceed without fear of nuclear consequence.[79]

The UK has made a non-use declaration. In 1978 and again in 1995 the British government stated that it would not use nuclear weapons against non-nuclear powers, with certain caveats:

> The United Kingdom will not use nuclear weapons against non-nuclear-weapon States Parties to the Treaty on the Non-Proliferation of Nuclear Weapons except in the case of an invasion or any other attack on the United Kingdom, its dependent territories, its armed forces, its Allies or on a State towards which it has a security commitment, carried out or sustained by such a non-nuclear-weapon State in association or alliance with a nuclear-weapon State.[80]

This Negative Security Assurance was reiterated in the 1998 SDR in rather less convoluted language.[81] France and the United States have made almost identical declarations. NSAs have been described as 'political theatre', useful but in no way determinants of future crisis behaviour. Like declarations of 'no first use', they are not, in one telling phrase, 'load-bearing'.[82]

Minimum deterrence

As well as not threatening non-nuclear states, Britain also tries to make its nuclear weapons as unthreatening as possible, emphasising their purely last-resort, deterrent nature. This is achieved through the notion of 'minimum deterrent'.[83] This is a legacy of the Cold War 'deterrence of the strong by the weak', a result of the finite resources the UK is able and willing to devote to nuclear armaments, and reflects the British view that nuclear weapons are a 'regrettable necessity'. France and China have both maintained minimum deterrents as well, though on a somewhat larger scale then the UK.[84] The advantage of a minimum deterrent is that force levels can be set by the requirements of minimal deterrence, rather than in relation to the arsenals of other states. The key question, then, is how much is enough? What force level (and type) will achieve the desired deterrent effect? The Moscow Criteria encapsulated this approach, the scope of the *Chevaline* system being dictated by the nature of the target and its defences, rather than in comparison to the Soviet ability to strike the UK.

Calculating the required scale and nature of a minimum deterrent can be difficult. If deterrence simply requires the threatening of a certain number of cities, it should be fairly straightforward. But if proportionality and credibility in the second nuclear age require more selective targeting, and the identity of future deterrees is uncertain, it is much less clear how an adequate 'minimum' force can be devised. While numbers can be kept at low levels, warhead yields and the means of their delivery may need to be fairly diverse. *Trident* meets the first of these requirements, but not all of the second. Quinlan cautions against *too* minimal an approach: 'if nuclear armouries are to exist at all, it is foolish to damage their deterrent utility by endless pruning at the margin'.[85] The British government's announcement that the number of 'operationally available' warheads was to be further reduced from 'fewer than 200' (the 1998 SDR) to 'fewer than 160' (the December 2006 White Paper) perhaps needs to be viewed in this light, though 'up to' 48 warheads on about 12 missiles in the submarine on patrol still represents a formidable capability.

Another legacy of Britain's Cold-War deterrence policy is the notion of the UK as an 'independent centre of decision-making'.[86] Previously known as the 'second' centre of decision-making, in an Alliance context, 'separately controlled but mutually supporting nuclear forces ... create an enhanced overall deterrent effect'. There had been little mention of the concept since the end of the Cold War, and in 1997 Quinlan stated that it was less cogent than it used to be.[87] Its inclusion in the December 2006 White Paper may be little more than an additional justification for retaining the deterrent.

The historical importance to Britain of the American nuclear guarantee has already been noted. Britain's modest nuclear force served both to influence the workings of this 'extended deterrence' and to insure against its failure. Often overlooked has been the UK's own extended deterrence on behalf of NATO allies, though it was re-stated in the 2006 White Paper:

'we would only consider using nuclear weapons in self-defence (including the defence of our NATO allies)'.[88] This is formally recognised in NATO's 1999 Strategic Concept: 'the independent nuclear forces of the United Kingdom and France ... contribute to the overall deterrence and security of the Allies'.[89]

More minimal postures than the minimum deterrent have sometimes been suggested, as further moves towards eventual nuclear disarmament and as confidence-building measures. Submarines could be taken off patrol, possibly with warheads removed from the missiles. Britain could even give up an operational capability altogether, while retaining the ability to re-constitute a nuclear force if required. Such policies are sometimes called 'virtual deterrence'.[90] These options are explicitly rejected by the current British government: 'any move from a dormant programme towards an active one could be seen as escalatory, and thus potentially destabilising, in a crisis'. The maintenance of a submarine always at sea is needed to assure its invulnerability and to remove an incentive for a pre-emptive attack.[91]

Nuclear defence

The British approach to nuclear deterrence has always been based on inflicting 'punishment' on an aggressor.[92] Faced by the Soviet Union, there was no alternative approach, as effective defence was impossible. But there are two principal forms of deterrence. Punishment threatens a response, the cost of which outweighs any gains from the original action. However, deterrence by denial instead aims to defeat the initial action itself, preventing the realisation of gain. Denial promises resistance, punishment retaliation. Both can be effective and need not be mutually exclusive. In the nuclear age denial is a good deal more demanding than punishment.[93] It is one thing to threaten to hit back, but quite another to be able to ward off the initial blow.

A strategy of deterrence by denial, if feasible, has some attractions. It imposes a degree of physical control that is lacking if one is simply testing the opponent's will to absorb retaliatory punishment.[94] It side-steps the intractable issue of proportionality. Denial does not suffer from the same crisis of credibility, as a willingness to defend oneself is inherently more believable than a readiness to punish others (many of them innocent bystanders with no responsibility for the original aggression). Denial capabilities also act as a hedge against deterrence failure.[95] Deterrence by denial has its own credibility challenge, however. Can it be effective when the consequences of even a few successful nuclear strikes would be so horrendous?

During the Cold War, deterrence and defence (or punishment and denial) were, in the main, seen as mutually exclusive. In the face of large-scale nuclear threats, defences had little to offer as an alternative to a threat of retaliation. They might, however, upset a 'stable' strategic balance based on assured vulnerability. After giving up on its own attempts to develop defences (on technical and cost grounds) in the 1950s, Britain became a particularly vociferous opponent of missile defence, for the simple reason that while defences could never undermine the huge superpower offensive arsenals, they could pose a severe problem for minimum deterrents like that of the British.[96] The *Chevaline* programme was designed to address just this problem.

In the second nuclear age there is no bipolar superpower nuclear stand-off. Nuclear threats and deterrence requirements are less severe but more diverse. Despite a residual attachment to an ill-defined 'strategic stability', since the demise of the ABM Treaty in 2002 British official attitudes towards 'active' missile defences have become a good deal more positive. The 2006 White Paper views them as 'complementary to other forms of defence or response, potentially reinforcing nuclear deterrence rather than superseding it'.[97]

With the exception of Russia's still-major capability, missile-borne nuclear threats in the future are likely to be far more modest in number, and much less sophisticated, than during the latter half of the Cold War.[98] Technological advances, especially in sensing and computing, make effective defences against small-scale missile attacks increasingly feasible. Offensive ballistic missiles need no longer enjoy the 'free ride'[99] long denied to other delivery systems such as aircraft, cruise missiles and terrorists. In the United States, the new strategic triad reflects the view that defensive, as well as offensive, systems can contribute to deterrence.

Integration of defences (denial) into a deterrence posture offers several advantages, especially in circumstances where traditional deterrence (punishment) may be weak.[100] By providing an alternative to automatic retaliation, defences could raise the nuclear threshold.[101] Where an opponent may have cause (rightly or wrongly) to doubt one's determination to retaliate, an ability to defeat a limited missile attack provides a second rationale for not mounting one. And given Western reluctance to countenance large-scale civilian casualties (as well as enemy casualties), the ability to defeat rather than to avenge an attack has obvious attractions. If deterrence should fail altogether, defences (both active and passive) can at least limit the consequences.[102] In the case of regional intervention by Western forces, a tactical defence against conventionally or WMD-armed missiles for deployed troops provides a more credible answer than a threat to conduct a nuclear strike with its inevitable consequences.[103] A strategic missile defence would similarly protect the domestic population from reprisals. Western governments might, therefore, have greater freedom of action.[104]

Thus far, British action on missile defence has been confined to a series of national and NATO studies, and granting permission for the use of the early-warning radar at Fylingdales for American missile defence.[105] British opposition to missile defence has been replaced by consent, but not yet by active participation, which would carry significant resource implications.

Deterrence uncertainty

Discussion of defence against nuclear or other WMD attack prompts the question of the reliability of deterrence. If deterrence is truly dependable, there is little need for an insurance against its failure, except in the sense of denial as well as punishment strands. If the world could survive 40 years of the Cold War without deterrence failure, perhaps we should be optimistic about the future.[106] However, if we know that nuclear deterrence has never failed, we can be less sure that it has always worked. Perhaps we were more lucky than skilful.[107]

A successful outcome to a deterrent relationship (in other words, the non-use of nuclear weapons) depends upon the way in which the parties involved interact. Profound differences exist in countries' leaderships, decision-making structures and processes, tolerance of risk and cost, perceptions, values and interests. All states are subject to a tendency towards wishful thinking and a propensity for gathering incomplete evidence about others' intentions to fit preconceived beliefs. It is quite possible to behave rationally within one's own parameters, yet act in ways that to others are incomprehensible or, importantly, unpredictable.[108] Not all rationalities are the same. Freedman advises us not to base deterrence on assumptions of rationality *or* stupidity.[109] Given the asymmetrical nature of deterrence relationships, what constitutes either rationality or stupidity is in the eye of the beholder. We simply cannot assume that others will behave in exactly the way we would, were we in their position. In particular, Western secular and pragmatic norms are not universal.[110]

In the absence of a known enemy against whom to plan, devising deterrent strategies for the future is fraught with difficulty. This is probably why, in the British government's 2006 White Paper section on 'Nuclear Deterrence in the 21st Century', more is said to justify the retention of the deterrent, than about nuclear-weapons doctrine. While the paper does say that the fundamentals of nuclear deterrence have not changed since the end of the Cold War,[111] the analysis here indicates that that may only be partially true, especially now that the UK has been freed from the demanding requirement to deter a nuclear superpower.

The United Kingdom must continue to respond to a highly unpredictable world in which nuclear weapons exist, where nuclear threats are likely to be less serious, but more diverse, than in the past. In that sense, deterrence requirements have become *more* demanding. Britain's reduction of both the numbers and types of weapons it deploys will make it all the more difficult to match future deterrence needs with appropriate tools.

Nuclear existentialism alone is insufficient if, when required, nuclear weapons are to act as an effective deterrent to threats to vital national interests. But declaring in advance the occasions when the UK might consider a nuclear response is both impossible (in view of an uncertain future) and undesirable (in view of the advantages of studied ambiguity). It does mean that 'useable' weapons (with relatively low yields and high accuracy) are required if deterrent threats are to be credible.

We should not take too much comfort from the fact that, so far, nuclear deterrence has never failed. One day it might; some argue it will. Wherever it might occur nuclear use will be a catastrophe, but that should not prevent policy-makers from thinking through how best to deal with it. Defences (at least defences against ballistic delivery systems), hitherto shunned by the UK, have an important role both in reinforcing deterrence and mitigating its potential failure. As Gray advises, the best we can do is to shorten the odds on the success of deterrence.[112]

CHAPTER FOUR

Nuclear Non-Proliferation

Britain's contemporary policy of nuclear deterrence is a response to nuclear proliferation. If nuclear weapons were not proliferated, and if existing holdings were being reduced to zero, the principal rationale for the UK's retention of a nuclear deterrent would be removed. This produces an immediate tension in policy towards nuclear weapons: some call it hypocrisy.[1] Britain, like the other NPT NWS, retains nuclear weapons while trying to prevent others from acquiring their own. By limiting the spread of nuclear weapons, the range of threats that the UK has to deter is kept as small as possible, and the chances of deterrence failing and nuclear weapons being used are reduced.

Deterrence and non-proliferation are sometimes viewed as mutually exclusive alternatives.[2] Up to a point, that is true. If non-proliferation (and, ultimately, disarmament) were completely successful, there would be no nuclear threats left to deter. But nuclear disarmament remains a distant and unlikely prospect. Deterrence deals with the existence of potential nuclear threats, while non-proliferation tries to reduce them.

The 2006 White Paper contains an annex which briefly outlines the UK's non-proliferation efforts. This suggests that, having decided to retain and update its nuclear capability, the British government is seeking to soften the blow by demonstrating its non-proliferation virtues. The paper strikes a 'balance' between a long-term commitment to a nuclear-free world and the protection of UK citizens.[3] Provision of the nuclear deterrent is the responsibility of the MoD. Diplomatic measures such as non-proliferation fall primarily under the remit of the Foreign and Commonwealth Office. That deterrence and non-proliferation should be separate policy areas is natural. But they seek to deal, by different means, with the same problem.

Deterrence and non-proliferation are inextricably linked. Philip Bobbitt says that 'deterrence is a key to nonproliferation'.[4] Michael Krepon calls them 'joined at the hip'.[5] During the Cold War, arms control helped to ensure that mutual deterrence worked. In turn, the extended deterrence provided by the United States to allies such as Germany and Japan removed a compelling incentive for them to acquire their own weapons.

The desire for non-proliferation is expressed principally through a series of arms-control treaties. Most of them originated during the Cold War as a means of limiting and stabilising the superpower nuclear arms race. With the end of the Cold War many have been overtaken by events. The Strategic Arms Limitation Treaties were followed by the Strategic Arms Reduction Treaties. They allowed the Cold War rivals higher numbers of strategic nuclear weapons than either now possesses. The 1987 Intermediate-range Nuclear Forces Treaty removed a whole category of weapons several years before the Soviet/Russian withdrawal from Europe would have had much the same effect. The ABM Treaty became defunct once the Americans withdrew from it in 2002. Today the Cold-War 'strategic balance' which these treaties enshrined has become irrelevant.[6]

The centrepiece of arms control measures surviving from the Cold War is the NPT, which codified the nuclear status of 1968 – five states with established nuclear arsenals and more than 180 states that agreed not to acquire them. There were predictions that by the end of the twentieth century there would be 20 or more states with nuclear arms.[7] The century actually ended with just three additional nuclear powers (Israel, India and Pakistan, none of them NPT signatories). To what extent this was a result of the NPT is a matter for counterfactual speculation, as much as is the role of nuclear deterrence in preventing the Cold War from becoming a nuclear war. The NPT has survived and retains its relevance because nuclear proliferation has replaced the old superpower arms race as the dominant nuclear arms-control issue. The NPT is a multilateral agreement and, therefore, still pertinent to today's diverse nuclear scene.

Most of the other Cold War arms-control treaties were bilateral US–Soviet agreements. Then, as now, the British (and French and Chinese) strategic nuclear forces remained outside negotiated reductions, as being 'minimal' they could not be reduced significantly without disappearing altogether.[8] Nevertheless, in the UK's case the acceptable minimum has been repeatedly reduced. Ironically, given the UK's public commitment to the arms-control process, the British nuclear reductions have been made unilaterally rather than by international agreement.

Gray tells us bluntly that 'arms are not the problem; rather it is the political demand for arms'.[9] States are armed because they distrust each other, not the other way round. Nor is arms control (a process) the same as the control of arms (the intended result). If measures of non-proliferation are to be successful in the second nuclear age, they will need to address the demand for, as well as the supply of, nuclear arms. This is a much more challenging requirement than in the so-called 'golden age' of arms control in the latter half of the Cold War, when arms control was focused on regularising the US–Soviet nuclear competition, though that was usually difficult enough.

It has been asserted that events like the demise of the ABM Treaty, alleged US rejection of multilateralism and the failure of the 2005 review of the NPT represent a 'descent into disorder'.[10] This is to focus unduly on the process rather than the outcome of non-proliferation. Arms-control treaties are useful and relevant not in themselves, but to the extent that they contribute to the slowing or reversal of proliferation and, even more importantly, the continued prospects for nuclear non-use.

The NPT

An international treaty is not the only way to retard the spread of nuclear weapons, but it should play a significant role. It can do so in two ways: by imposing legal and physical constraints on proliferation; and by 'de-legitimising', and thus deterring, the acquisition of nuclear weapons by states that have foresworn them. Since its inception in the late 1960s, the non-proliferation regime represented by the NPT has acquired a near-universal totemic status that in itself enhances its effectiveness. With the exception of the three states that have never come within in its scope (Israel, India and Pakistan) and one that withdrew from the treaty (North Korea) all other countries, publicly at least, frame their nuclear policies with reference to the NPT regime. This is so whether they retain, or resist acquiring, nuclear weapons.

However, there are some fundamental weaknesses in the NPT. The 'nuclear apartheid' which it formalises represents the nuclear status quo of nearly 40 years ago. It may not have become irrelevant in the way the ABM Treaty did, but with the passage of time its structure has become somewhat less relevant to contemporary circumstances. Its 'grand bargain'[11] between nuclear and non-nuclear states has become strained for two reasons. First, the Article VI commitment to nuclear disarmament remains as much a distant aspiration as it has ever been, but its presence in the treaty continues to act as a distraction that can inhibit practical cooperation to limit proliferation. Secondly, non-nuclear-weapon states were given access to civil nuclear technology, much of which has a potential military application, a fact not fully understood at the time of the treaty's signing.[12]

The fundamental problem with any such agreement is that states sign it when it is perceived to serve their interests, and may observe its provisions only so long as it continues to do so. Like declarations of no first use, treaty obligations will count for little when vital national interests are at stake, which is precisely when the possession and use of nuclear weapons will be relevant. It must be acknowledged, though, that an existing formal diplomatic commitment will be an important factor in any calculation about national interest. This has led to predictions that the NPT regime is bound, sooner or later, to collapse.[13] It is certainly under pressure, not least because it has not prevented a former member, North Korea, from acquiring at least a primitive weapon capability and it may be unable to stop another party to the treaty, Iran, from ultimately doing so as well.

The NPT provides a means whereby the non-nuclear states can put pressure on the five NWS in the direction of eventual nuclear disarmament. It also gives the NWS a legal and diplomatic lever to use on proliferating states. The treaty sanctions nuclear ownership by the NWS, but no one else. While the 'hypocrisy' of the NWS is self-evident, it is enshrined in the very treaty, ratified by more states than any other in history, which permits them, and them alone, to possess nuclear weapons.

The NPT survives because it continues to serve the interests of the overwhelming majority of its signatories. The legitimation of the five NWS serves not only their own interests, but also those of states benefiting from extended deterrence – including all the other NATO countries and US allies in Asia such as Japan and South Korea. Elsewhere, the NPT reassures states that while they live in a nuclear-armed world, they at least will not have to engage in local nuclear competitions. That the NPT continues to serve most states' national interests was demonstrated in 1995, when the treaty was extended indefinitely.[14]

As one of the five NWS, the UK's attitude towards the treaty is necessarily ambivalent. On the one hand, as the 1998 SDR put it, 'this Treaty is the cornerstone of the international non-proliferation regime and the essential foundation for the pursuit of nuclear disarmament'.[15] On the other hand, the British government has decided to extend the life of its nuclear capability until at least the 2040s.[16] The 2006 White Paper's annex dealing with the UK's non-proliferation efforts makes no mention of the NPT, though an accompanying fact sheet stresses that the UK is 'fully compliant with all our NPT obligations'.[17]

While it can be argued that renewing the deterrent breaches at least the spirit of the treaty, the NPT does not require a unilateral action on the part of the UK, nor does the treaty set any timescale for general nuclear disarmament.[18] The latter is to take place in the context of 'general and complete disarmament', towards which all states have made much less progress than have the NWS in terms of nuclear disarmament.[19] This situation is not materially changed by the more forceful disarmament commitment made at the NPT's 2000 review conference.[20]

Nonetheless, the NPT does commit the five NWS to eventual nuclear disarmament. This was part of the original grand bargain, but with serious arms-control negotiations barely underway between the United States and the Soviet Union, it was more of a gesture than a statement of actual intent. Nuclear abolition looks no more likely today than it did then. But it remains a formal commitment, and one that the British government routinely reiterates whenever discussing nuclear policy. The 2006 White Paper states that 'we stand by our unequivocal undertaking to accomplish the total elimination of nuclear weapons'.[21] But nuclear disarmament is not a matter for practical policy-making and efforts to achieve it might have dangerous consequences: 'in the world of the "non-nuclear" the "just-nuclear" would be king'.[22] Though this situation will always be deeply unsatisfactory, even immoral for some, complete nuclear disarmament remains no more than a vague, open-ended aspiration. In the meantime, the NPT does serve to stigmatise the possession of nuclear weapons, influencing states that have them to make reductions while inhibiting others from acquiring them.[23] The awkwardness for the UK of the NPT's long-term aspiration of nuclear disarmament is, therefore, apparently outweighed by its more immediate role in reducing the scale of proliferation with which the deterrent might have to deal.

Wider efforts

Nuclear non-proliferation measures are not confined to the NPT and the UK is a party to several other treaties dealing with WMD. These include the Comprehensive Test Ban Treaty (CTBT), the Nuclear Suppliers' Group and the Missile Technology Control Regime. Britain played important roles in negotiating many of these agreements.[24] The 2006 White Paper summarises several other non-proliferation activities.[25] With the notable exception of the CTBT, few of these prohibit the UK from doing something it might otherwise wish to.

The CTBT was signed in 1998, and Britain and France were the first NWS to ratify it. The United States has not done so, but continues to observe its provisions. Britain has not conducted a nuclear test since 1991. A new warhead might be required for *Trident* in the 2020s,[26] which in the past would have required testing in order to verify its performance, safety and reliability. Adherence to the CTBT forecloses this option, and withdrawal from it is not provided for (unlike, for example, the old ABM Treaty). The UK's ability to maintain its existing warheads and, when required, to produce a replacement without conducting a test is being addressed by the continuing upgrading of facilities at Aldermaston.

A Fissile Material Cut-off Treaty (FMCT), which would ban the world-wide production of separated plutonium and highly enriched uranium, has been under discussion at the UN Conference on Disarmament for some years. Britain, like the other NWS, already has access to sufficient fissile material so the FMCT, if effective, would serve non-proliferation without significantly inhibiting the UK's own weapons programme.[27]

The Proliferation Security Initiative (PSI) is a new kind of measure to curb proliferation. The US government established the PSI in 2003, partly as a response to North Korean transfers of weapons to other states.[28] Britain is one of 15 other 'core nations'. The PSI makes provision for the interdiction (mainly at sea) of WMD and their delivery systems, and the exchange of intelligence to support these activities. It is not a complete solution to the risks of transfers between proliferating states, but may prove to be a significant tool in containing the problem.[29]

The transfer of WMD technologies to non-state actors is addressed by UN Security Council Resolution 1540, adopted in April 2004. The resolution places legally binding obligations on states to establish effective physical controls on WMD-related materials, and to report accordingly: 'henceforth, they cannot escape a duty of internal care'.[30] Like the proposed FMCT and the PSI, UNSC 1540 does not oblige the UK to act in ways it would not otherwise, but it may help to restrict the further spread of WMD.

One reason, though not the only one, for believing that a nuclear-free world may be impossible to achieve is the problem of verification. No system of verification is likely to prove faultless, and there will always be temptations for a state to cheat. Nuclear possession in an otherwise nuclear-free world would give the state in question unique leverage, as the United States found in 1945. Even without wanting to cheat as such, the prudent state will always assume that others might do so, and will want to hedge against that possibility. Possession of nuclear weapons today is, after all, a hedge against possession by others.

That does not mean that verification is pointless. Like the PSI and UNSC 1540, it is no 'silver bullet' but is a useful tool in containing proliferation. The UK is at the forefront of practical verification efforts.[31] Some of this activity is conducted by the same institution that maintains the UK's own weapons capability – AWE, which conducts seismic monitoring and analysis of suspected nuclear tests.[32] This neatly illustrates the UK's 'twin-track' policy of maintaining its own nuclear weapons while trying to deny them to others.

Diplomatic activities aimed at particular countries may also be effective. The UK-initiated Anglo-American engagement of Libya, previously regarded as an international pariah, has been successful in taking the country off the list of would-be nuclear proliferants. Long-term sanctions and quiet diplomacy eventually yielded the desired result.[33]

Diplomacy is proving much less successful with Iran. In this case, the UK has joined France and Germany (the 'EU3') to negotiate with Tehran. But Iran has a more advanced nuclear programme than Libya had, has much greater resources, is not subject to a universal sanctions regime and is more determined to pursue its own security agenda.[34] Security assurances have not proved sufficient to persuade Iran that it does not need a nuclear capability, not least because of its wish to deter intervention by the United States and to confront Israel.[35] Iran's future nuclear capability and uncertain political direction probably provides one specific rationale for a UK nuclear deterrent.

Proliferation and non-proliferation

Containment is perhaps an apt description of the entire regime of non-proliferation instruments. The prospects for complete nuclear disarmament are as remote as ever. But limiting, so far as possible, further proliferation is a worthwhile effort. Fortunately, after Iran there are few extra, if any, candidates for nuclear status in the short term.[36] In the longer term, the most likely regions for further proliferation are in East Asia and in the Middle East. In both cases, this is likely to be in response to existing proliferants – North Korea and Iran, respectively. When and if further proliferation occurs in these areas will be crucially affected by the relationship between regional states' concerns and the engagement of the United States, especially through extended deterrence.[37]

Some argue that recent and ongoing proliferation is a response, not to established nuclear arsenals, but to the superior *conventional* capabilities of Western countries, especially the United States.[38] This is true insofar as external actors play a role in regional proliferation. However, Western states like the UK should not overestimate the extent to which they are a spur to proliferation, or what they can usefully do to prevent it. Strictly regional security requirements may be crucial (as, for example, in the case of India and Pakistan) and so may be the internal dynamics of particular regimes (for example, Iran).

The UK has a very full, active and diverse programme of non-proliferation activities, which, despite the country's continued possession of nuclear weapons, has won international plaudits.[39] Non-proliferation measures can never solve all of the world's nuclear ills, but they can only help.

Jonathan Schell, among others, argues that combining the possession of nuclear weapons with efforts to curb proliferation is a policy that lacks coherence,[40] and, logically speaking, that must be true. But as a practical response to the continued existence of nuclear weapons, the maintenance of a deterrent and an active non-proliferation policy ought to be, not mutually exclusive, but mutually reinforcing.

CHAPTER FIVE

Future Nuclear Capability

The British government's December 2006 White Paper makes it clear that, as widely expected, the UK is to retain a nuclear deterrent. Having decided to remain in the nuclear-weapons business, the next question concerns the nature of the successor deterrent. This decision has also been taken, though some details remain to be determined. These decisions are still subject to parliamentary scrutiny, and significant expenditure will not begin until around 2012,[1] at least one General Election hence. A future British government could always reverse or modify current policy. But it is extremely unlikely that, in the short term at least, the UK will proceed on any basis other than the one currently set out by the government.

Having committed itself to retaining a deterrent, the most important decision for the British government concerns the type of deterrent it wants for the future. Though there must always be a presumption in favour of keeping the same kind of system, before committing significant resources it is appropriate, as with any military capability, to examine alternative ways of achieving the same effect. The White Paper examines four 'generic' options in some detail:

- Long-range aircraft (converted civil airliners) equipped with air-launched cruise missiles;
- Large surface ships carrying adapted *Trident* ballistic missiles;
- A land-based silo system, also with appropriately adapted *Tridents*;
- New SSBNs with *Trident*.

Other options, such as short-range aircraft or a ballistic missile other than *Trident* D5, were dismissed as either inadequate or too costly and risky.[2] The possibility of submarine-launched cruise missiles is mentioned as a variation on the first and last of the above four options, and this configuration has been widely viewed as the most promising alternative to the existing SSBN–SLBM combination.[3] In 1977, Smart conducted a detailed, open-source examination for Chatham House of the options for a *Polaris* successor.[4] He concluded, in the Cold War context, that the best technical options were submarine-launched ballistic or cruise missiles. *For a similar deterrent effect* the latter was considerably more expensive, mainly because much larger numbers of missiles and submarines were required.

The Cold War imperative to deter Moscow has gone (at least for the present). But some requirements from that time do remain, albeit in a more generalised form. The launch platform must remain invulnerable to pre-emptive attack[5] and the delivery system must be able to penetrate defences.[6] These are two basic requirements of any credible deterrent capability. To these is now added the additional criteria of being able to deter threats anywhere in the world,[7] which implies a combination of platform and delivery system that can reach anywhere in the world.

Cruise missiles are rejected in the 2006 White Paper on the grounds that they lack the necessary range, speed and payload.[8] The options of placing *Trident* missiles in land-based silos or on large surface ships are dismissed on the grounds of greater vulnerability, reduced reach and at least equal cost, so 'from a capability perspective ... a submarine-based system offers the most practical and effective means of meeting our future nuclear deterrence requirements'.[9] This conclusion and the analysis of alternatives that underpins it are supported by several independent analyses.[10]

What, then, will a future *Trident*-based deterrent look like? Like the present system, it will necessarily comprise four main elements: the nuclear warheads; the missiles; the submarine platforms; and the supporting infrastructure for each of the other three elements. The defining component is the missiles. Warheads must be compatible with the available delivery system, *Trident*, and the submarines must in turn be compatible with *Trident*. It is, therefore, logical to examine the missiles first.

The missiles

The option of extending the life of the *Trident* system exists only because the United States has already decided to do so. Fourteen of the US Navy's *Ohio*-class submarines are having their service lives extended – the last of the class will be decommissioned in 2042. In 2002, Lockheed Martin was awarded a contract to extend the lives of US Navy *Trident* D5 missiles to match this timescale. This will entail replacing certain components, mainly those that represent obsolescent technology and are becoming unsupportable.[11] The Mk 4 re-entry vehicle (as used by the UK) will similarly have its service life extended. The British MoD insists that refurbishment does not entail any improvement in capability in terms of payload, range or accuracy.[12]

In the 1970s the British government decided to upgrade and extend the life of the existing system, *Polaris*, even though the Americans were not doing the same. This time, the United States *is* extending the life of an existing system rather than acquiring a new one. Britain could again fall out of step if it were not to upgrade its share of the common *Trident* pool – indeed after a time it would cease to be a common pool. The lessons from the *Chevaline* programme in terms of the technical risk and increased cost in 'going it alone' remain applicable.

The American decision means that if Britain is to keep SLBMs it needs to follow the same route. It is sometimes suggested that the UK could instead purchase French M-51 missiles, but these have a larger diameter, would require wholly new warheads to fit them, are less accurate, and would end the long and hitherto happy practice of cooperation with the United States. Nowhere in the 2006 White Paper is this option even mentioned, and it is severely curtailed by existing undertakings made to the US.

It has been assumed that the need to replace not the missiles but the submarines is the driving factor in decisions on *Trident*'s future.[13] However, the White Paper states simply that a decision as to whether or not the UK should participate in the missile life-extension programme is required in 2007, but does not elaborate on the subject. Presumably long-term planning and contractual arrangements in the United States give the UK only a limited opportunity to join the programme. Firm orders for new submarines will clearly not be placed for some years, but a commitment to the missile programme is apparently needed now. In that sense, the missiles *are* the key driver in present decision timescales.

The UK currently holds title to 50 missiles, and does not plan to purchase additional *Tridents*.[14] It has decided to participate in the missile life-extension programme at a cost of £250m (£5m per weapon), with the first of the modified missiles entering Royal Navy service in a little over 10 years' time.[15]

The government is no more open in the recent White Paper than in previous statements about the number of missiles actually deployed in a submarine on patrol. There are normally three submarines in commission, with missiles loaded. As the UK's remaining stockpile of 50 includes spares and weapons allocated for test-firings, it is clear that fewer than the possible 16 are actually carried. An assumption of 12 per boat is probably reasonable. The government's reticence is surprising given that it is much more forthcoming about the number of warheads carried, which objectively ought to be a more sensitive subject.

The *Trident* life-extension programme will keep the system operational until the early 2040s. By that time the new submarines will only be between 12 and 20 years old. If the deterrent is to be maintained beyond that point either a wholly new system will need to be procured (wasting several years of life remaining in the submarines), or the replacement for *Trident* will have to be retro-fitted to the existing platforms. American plans for the sea-based element of their nuclear deterrent will determine what options are available to the UK.

The US Navy intends to introduce a new SSBN from 2029 onwards and thereafter at a rate of one per year to replace the entire 14-boat force by 2042.[16] A new missile will need to be in service by 2029 to equip the first of the new submarines. The UK has already received assurances from the US government that this missile will be made available to the UK, and that it will be compatible with the *Trident* launch system.[17] It will, therefore, be suitable for the new *Trident* submarines.

This undertaking was one of the more surprising aspects of the 2006 White Paper. However, it must already be clear to the US Navy that its requirements for a *Trident* replacement will lead to a weapon that looks very like *Trident*, which already meets all likely future needs in terms of range and payload, though improved accuracy would expand targeting options. One might speculate that *Trident* D5A (the extended-life version) will be replaced by a *Trident* D5B, D6 or E6. Even if the US develops a common SLBM–ICBM weapon, its design will be determined by the needs of submarine-launch. A possible submarine-launched intermediate-range ballistic missile has been studied but even this would be required to fit into a *Trident* tube.[18]

The exchange of letters between the prime minister and the president in December 2006 contains a further possibility, which is, curiously, left out of the White Paper. This would be a further life-extension of the D5 missile – for UK purposes – to match the out-of-service dates of the new submarines. If this course of action were to be chosen, it would be comparable to the time when *Polaris* was retained in UK service long after it had been discarded by the US. But it would re-synchronise the procurement of submarines and missiles, and might be favoured if at the time when a *Trident* D5A successor were chosen the government were unwilling to commit the UK to yet another generation of submarines to carry the *Trident* successor missile.

The de-linking of British procurement timescales for submarines and missiles does entail some risk. However, it has the advantage of a more incremental approach similar to that adopted by France, which spreads expenditure more evenly over a longer period rather than the 'peaks and troughs' characteristic of the British deterrent since the 1960s.

The warheads

The current warhead for the UK's *Trident* missiles is an 'anglicised' version, locally designed and built, of the US W-76 warhead. As *Trident* will continue to be the delivery system until the early 2040s there might be few immediate consequences for the warhead. In 2006, however, the government did announce that it would make a 20% cut in the number of 'operationally available' warheads, to fewer than 160. The additional, but undefined, margin will be cut by the same proportion.[19] This further reduction in the size of the minimum deterrent is not justified on any operational grounds, but as an example for others to follow.[20] It, therefore, meets non-proliferation and, perhaps, domestic political needs rather than strategic requirements. It leaves the UK with probably the smallest holdings of any of the five NPT NWS.

The existing warheads can be maintained in service into the 2020s, with some 'relatively minor upgrading and refurbishment',[21] which the current improvements at Aldermaston are designed to enable. One of the details about *Trident* life extension still to be determined is whether the warhead can be further extended in service, or whether a new one will be required. The government has not explained why it would not be possible to go on manufacturing new warheads in line with the present design, using existing stocks of fissile material. The cost of refurbishment or replacement of the warheads is put at £2–3bn,[22] in addition to the £1bn currently being spent to refurbish AWE Aldermaston itself.[23]

If a new warhead is to be developed, either for *Trident* or an eventual successor, the issue of testing arises. The UK has signed and ratified the CTBT. The US has signed the treaty and despite not ratifying it continues to observe its provisions. Since 2005 the United States has been developing a reliable replacement warhead (RRW).[24] The RRW is designed to ensure safety and reliability ('stockpile stewardship') without the need to conduct testing, while also trading the Cold-War imperatives of high yield and low weight for characteristics now more relevant such as lower cost, easier manufacture and reduced maintenance.

The RRW programme has many of the same aims as any British refurbishment and/or replacement of its *Trident* warheads. It must be of interest to the UK though for both diplomatic and domestic political reasons no British government will want to announce a new warhead programme until or unless absolutely necessary. Cooperation with the American programme has obvious attractions, and the US is reported to be interested in sharing costs and expertise.[25] The United States has not designed a new warhead any more recently than the UK.

The director-general, strategic technologies in the MoD has confirmed that Aldermaston retains the ability, if required, to design and build a new warhead.[26] The UK already has a choice of yields from the existing warhead. If a new one is needed, the opportunity could be taken to provide a wider range of probably smaller yields, thus expanding targeting options and enhancing deterrence credibility. Non-proliferation objectives could be furthered by announcing the maximum (but reduced) yield of the new weapon.

A little-noticed change in the 2006 White Paper was from '48' warheads per submarine to 'up to 48'.[27] This was apparently introduced in order to allow greater flexibility in missile/warhead loading – maintaining exactly 48 allows for relatively few combinations, though the often-assumed 16 missiles with three warheads each has *never* been deployed.[28] A reduction in the number of deployed warheads would also be consistent with the 20% cut in overall numbers.

The submarines

The principal catalyst for the current debate on the future of the nuclear deterrent is the need to replace the four *Vanguard*-class submarines, which entered operational service between 1994 and 2001. They have a design life of 25 years[29] so the first of class, HMS *Vanguard*, will be withdrawn from service in 2017[30] and the last, HMS *Vengeance*, around 2026. The MoD commissioned concept studies into possible future platforms for the *Trident* missile as early as May 2002.[31] These studies, which remain classified, were completed a year later and before the Defence White Paper published in December that year launched the public debate.[32] In July 2006 the government stated that it would take at least 14 years (the time it took for the *Vanguards*) to design, procure and deploy a new submarine.[33] By the end of the year that timescale had increased to 17 years,[34] probably as a result of experience with the *Astute*-class SSNs and a recognition that a wholly new design may be required.

It has already been noted that the US Navy is extending the lives of its equivalent (but different) *Ohio*-class boats quite substantially. A similar life-extension for the UK's submarines is not possible, as provision for it would have had to be designed into the class from the outset. A more modest life extension is possible, at some cost, which would take HMS *Vanguard* to about 2022.[35] The 2006 White Paper does not actually state that a limited life-extension programme will be undertaken, but that is the implication to be drawn from the timescales set out for eventual replacement.

Some commentary has suggested that the lifespan of the submarines is limited by the strains put upon the hulls.[36] In fact, the concern is reactor life, and not least the extremely stringent safety and regulatory regimes under which they are operated.[37] The nuclear steam-raising plant makes the UK's all-nuclear submarine fleet a unique national military platform which cannot be managed and operated like any other, and raises the difficult and expensive issue of the costs of 'nuclear ownership'. At the end of the Cold War, the Royal Navy operated 21 nuclear-powered submarines (4 SSBNs and 17 SSNs). The overall costs of nuclear ownership were spread over a relatively large number of hulls and the submarine industrial base (SIB), as it is now called, produced a new submarine every 12–18 months. Today there are just 13 submarines in service and that number could be further reduced to as few as ten. This would generate fewer orders for the SIB and make each individual boat considerably more expensive to build and operate.

The future of the SIB is itself a matter of concern, to the extent that the MoD commissioned a series of studies on the subject from RAND Europe.[38] The effects of reducing the number of submarines required have been exacerbated by problems with the new *Astute*-class, partly as a result of a large gap in submarine design and production in the 1990s and by new design methods.[39] The *Astute* programme, late and over budget, had become unaffordable.[40] It is now in better shape, but orders for more than the initial three boats have yet to be placed.[41] This is relevant to the future of the nuclear deterrent because, without an adequate and sustainable SIB, the UK will be unable to build new SSBNs. Conversely, without new SSBNs there would be inadequate numbers of SSN orders alone to sustain the SIB, and Britain will be unable to build an eventual replacement for the *Astute*-class. In addition, the SSNs and SSBNs share the same operating and maintenance bases. Their futures are inextricably linked, and it is possible that the new SSBNs will be the last nuclear-powered submarines built in Britain.[42]

For the foreseeable future, the government's Defence Industrial Strategy intends to 'retain all those capabilities unique to submarines and their Nuclear Steam Raising Plant, to enable their design, development, build, support, operation and decommissioning'.[43] Defence economist Keith Hartley summed up the special nature of the SIB as being crucial to the future of the nuclear deterrent:

> It specialises in one product, namely nuclear-powered submarines; there is only one buyer [the UK government]; there is only one supplier [BAE Systems Submarines]; it is wholly dependent on domestic orders; its order volume is small-scale; there are lengthy timescales for development and production; and there is a requirement for highly specialised support and test facilities that have no alternative use.[44]

The MoD plans to maintain a 'drumbeat' of submarine completions at 22-month intervals, including seven *Astutes* and the future SSBNs.[45] If sustained, this could (just) form the basis for a viable SIB. The industrial base was the subject of the House of Commons Defence Committee's second and very detailed report on the future of the nuclear deterrent.[46]

When the original *Vanguard*-class was being procured, the then-MoD Permanent Secretary Michael Quinlan suggested that just three boats would be sufficient.[47] It was decided, however, that the long-term maintenance of the CASD required a fourth submarine. One question left open in the 2006 White Paper is whether a new design and changes to operating and support arrangements might allow the building this time of just three new boats. A new reactor core ('Core H') that does not require refuelling during the life of the submarine will reduce the time spent in refit. However, a reduction to three platforms leaves less margin for mishap, will increase the cost of individual units and exacerbate the difficulty in sustaining the industrial base.

Probably easier to determine, though as yet still unresolved, will be the number of missile tubes the new submarines will carry. The present *Trident* submarines, like the *Polaris* boats before them, each have 16 tubes. Reductions in the number of missiles and warheads mean that not all missile tubes are used, and indeed consideration was given to equipping the *Vanguards* with only 12.[48] A reduction to 12 tubes in the new boats would make a very modest cost saving and provide a further gesture in the direction of nuclear disarmament. It probably would not reduce flexibility for the future, as the UK will only have a limited number of missiles available anyway.

There are three potential design options for a new submarine: an updated *Vanguard*; a 'stretched' *Astute*; or a wholly new design. No final decision has been taken on this, and the government's statements so far have been ambivalent. The 2006 White Paper talks of changes to the design of the *Vanguard*-class, but elsewhere discusses designing a new submarine and needing up to 17 years to bring it into service.[49] An updated *Vanguard* would clearly take much less time to develop.

The SSBN is designed around two key components – the missile section and the propulsion plant. The former is a known factor and would be common to all three solutions (the *Astute* design is of sufficient diameter to accommodate the *Trident* missile tubes). The *Vanguard* and *Astute* classes share the same propulsion system, the Pressurised Water Reactor (PWR) 2, whose design dates from the 1980s. The benefits of a proven design and commonality with existing submarine classes will have to be weighed against the potential size, weight and cost advantages of a new-generation propulsion system (which might include all-electric drive, greatly reducing the number of large mechanical parts).[50] Adaptation of either of the existing PWR 2-based designs risks building in future obsolescence and high running costs for a submarine that will be in service into the 2050s.[51] The MoD has already funded studies into a successor to the PWR 2;[52] this could also drive a future *Astute* replacement.

The December 2006 US–UK exchange of letters contains an agreement to 'explore the scope for cooperation and collaboration on other aspects of future submarine platforms'. It is unlikely that the UK would copy the future American SSBN design as the timescales for new submarines are different (2022 and 2029, respectively), but it may be able to draw on US expertise and assistance for which there are existing precedents.[53]

A so-called 'hybrid' SSN–SSBN design has been mooted. This would carry a smaller number of SLBM tubes and be able to launch conventionally armed cruise missiles.[54] A single submarine platform could be more cost-effective and flexible. However, the two roles are operationally incompatible and a single submarine could only perform one task at a time. Redundant capabilities would, therefore, be incorporated into each unit, and ambiguity as to a particular submarine's current role could undermine deterrence and add to crisis instability. There is no indication that the MoD has examined this idea in any detail.

The cost of four new SSBNs is put at £11–14bn at 2006–07 prices.[55] This figure appears to be high, given that the present four boats, at 2004–05 prices, cost about half that amount (£5.9bn).[56] The increase may reflect experience with *Astute* and the fact that with a smaller overall submarine-building programme, individual units become more expensive. There is also a determination within the MoD not to underestimate costs as any later over-runs would come at the expense of other elements of the its equipment programme.[57] If a four-boat force is to be maintained, the first new submarine is required in service to replace *Vanguard* in about 2022. Construction would, therefore, start in about 2016. A three-boat force could be introduced about two years later, with the second of the existing units, *Victorious*, being replaced in 2024.

Political issues and the future of the deterrent

Two further political issues impinge on the future of the nuclear deterrent. One is civil nuclear power, the other the 'Scottish question'.

The Royal Navy is not the UK's only operator of nuclear reactors. Britain built the world's first nuclear power station in the 1950s, and today nuclear energy supplies 22% of the country's energy.[58] However, no new nuclear stations have been built in Britain for almost 20 years and the older stations are now being decommissioned. Unless new stations are built, there will only be one site still operating by 2023, Sizewell B in Suffolk.[59] An ongoing government review of future energy needs indicates that with energy consumption increasing, supplies of oil and gas dwindling and concerns about global warming through the burning of fossil fuels, construction of new, more efficient nuclear stations is probably required. France generates 78% of its electricity from nuclear power stations.[60]

If the UK does not build new civil nuclear stations, the Royal Navy will eventually become the UK's only operator of nuclear reactors. Apart from the need to decommission existing reactors, the entire burden of the nuclear safety and regulatory regimes would fall on the defence budget.

Since 1998, Scotland has enjoyed a substantial measure of autonomy as a result of the so-called 'devolution settlement'. Coincidentally, in the same year *Trident* became the UK's sole nuclear-weapon system with the phasing out of the last WE 177 bombs. *Trident* submarines are operated from the naval base at Faslane, north of Glasgow, and their warheads are stored and loaded onto missiles at the nearby RNAD Coulport.[61] The rest of Britain's nuclear-weapons infrastructure is located south of the border in England, mainly at Barrow, Devonport, Derby, Aldermaston and Northwood.

Defence and foreign affairs are matters specifically reserved for the Westminster Parliament under the Scotland Act of 1998. However, operation of the nuclear bases in Scotland does depend on the active cooperation of several local authorities. Anti-nuclear sentiment is a good deal stronger in Scotland than in the rest of the UK, including within the Scottish Labour Party, the Scottish National Party (which advocates an independent Scotland) and the Scottish Churches.

Notwithstanding the Scotland Act, Scotland's future constitutional status is far from fully resolved. There remains a strong pro-independence movement in Scotland and there is also increasing resentment in England at undue Scottish influence in the UK parliament over what are, post-devolution, often purely English policy matters, as well as over higher levels of public spending in Scotland.[62] One may speculate as to whether the greatest threat to the Union comes from the Scots, or the English. Certainly, the future integrity of the United Kingdom can by no means be taken for granted. Elections to the Scottish Parliament will take place in May 2007 which could see the SNP become the largest party, committed to holding a referendum on independence.

An independent Scotland would have obvious implications for the nuclear deterrent. As by far the larger member of the union, England, following the precedent set by the break-up of the Soviet Union, would become the residual NWS under the terms of the NPT.[63] *Trident* subma-rines could only continue to operate from Scotland with the agreement of the (presumably anti-nuclear) Scottish government, yet without that government (under the terms of the NPT) having any say in its opera-tion. An independent Scotland might, therefore, have *less* influence over Scottish-based nuclear weapons than Westminster-based Scottish members of Parliament do today.

Alternatively, *Trident* might have to be relocated outside Scotland.[64] Other basing options were examined when *Polaris* was first acquired. One was in Milford Haven, but that would simply raise the Welsh question, and Milford Haven is a major oil terminal. The only likely alternative to Faslane and Coulport is Devonport (where the submarines are refitted anyway), with a new RNAD at Falmouth. The political difficulties of relocating nuclear weapons aside, this would clearly be a costly business.[65]

The building, maintenance and operation of a much-reduced nuclear submarine force is divided among more sites than is ideal. The boats are built at Barrow, refitted at Devonport and operate from Faslane. All three sites have to be nuclear-certified, a complex and expensive business. Moreover, since 1997 the overall size of the Royal Navy has been substan-tially reduced and may not be large enough to warrant the retention of its present three operating bases at Faslane, Devonport and Portsmouth. The Scottish question might suggest the closure of Faslane, but existing invest-ment there will probably secure its future. For the moment, consolidation of the nuclear infrastructure will occur across existing sites rather than by reducing the number of them.[66]

The futures of *Trident* and Faslane are inextricably linked. But the Scottish question will ensure that both remain on the political agenda even after *Trident* has been modernised and its life extended.

CONCLUSIONS

The future will be nuclear. Not only can nuclear weapons not be disinvented, but efforts to seek their elimination are bound to fail. This inevitable reality creates a difficult dilemma: how to convince those states that have so far opted not to acquire nuclear weapons that their interests are best secured by continuing this course even while others insist that they must maintain the nuclear capabilities they currently possess? There is no escape from this dilemma – neither promises nor demands that nuclear weapons eventually be eliminated can be fulfilled. Any expectation to the contrary is a cruel illusion.[1]

Though it continues to pay lip-service to eventual and complete nuclear disarmament, the British government apparently shares this nuclear pessimism. It is certainly proceeding on the basis that in a partially nuclear-armed world, it is better to have than to have not. Tony Blair told the House of Commons 'it would be unwise and dangerous for Britain, alone of the nuclear powers, to give up its independent deterrent'.[2] To no-one's surprise the Blair government has decided to extend the life of the UK's *Trident*-based nuclear deterrent, while at the same time remaining at the forefront of efforts to curb further nuclear proliferation.

There seems to be near-universal agreement that if the UK did not already possess nuclear weapons, in today's circumstances it would not be seeking to acquire them.[3] But Britain has had them for more than half a century and to give them up now, whatever the financial, diplomatic and moral temptations, would be an unwarranted gamble. The only thing we do know about the future is that it is uncertain. Possession of nuclear weapons will be the answer to very few of the security challenges that lie ahead. But it might just be the answer to the security challenge that really matters – the threat of nuclear attack.

The recent public debate and the parallel government decision have been about the maintenance of the status quo. It has been a continuation decision rather than a replacement decision.[4] There is to be no change in British policy towards nuclear weapons, either its own or those of others. The sum that needs to be spent to sustain the status quo is, in absolute terms, considerable, but in relative terms much less so. The government's decision and the accompanying debate have provided an opportunity to conduct a review and update of British nuclear-weapons policy which has established greater, though partial, transparency than before.

Other than financial savings, the arguments in favour of abandoning nuclear weapons have related to Britain's obligations under the NPT, and the perceived boost to non-proliferation that such a gesture would provide. Neither case is at all convincing. The legal position is at best ambivalent and the relevance of legal judgements to matters of ultimate national security is questionable. The effect that a self-denying example set by Britain would have on others is likely to be slight.

Gray judges that 'the issue of Britain as a NWS is unusual in that all of the merit lies on one side of the argument, the case for Britain remaining a NWS'.[5] That statement no doubt offends many proponents of unilateral nuclear disarmament, but there is no indication that the current British government has even contemplated not retaining its nuclear weapons.

The most widespread concern, including within military circles, is the opportunity cost of a decision to spend between £15 and £20bn. The proportion of GDP spent on defence has almost halved in the last 15 years, yet operational commitments have increased substantially. The MoD has been at pains to emphasise the special nature of nuclear weapons and their lack of strict military utility. The government, sensitive to the issue, promises that funding for *Trident* renewal will not be at the expense of conventional capabilities.[6] It has been mooted that spending on *Trident* could be met from within a special reserve or contingency fund outside the defence budget.[7] This does not, however, accord with the realities of government budgeting processes, and it only go so far as to say that spending decisions on both nuclear and conventional forces will be taken as part of the 2007 Comprehensive Spending Review.[8] Many observers will view that statement with suspicion, particularly the Navy, which fears being reduced, in effect, to the status of a nuclear-armed coastguard.

Trident was designed and bought in a very different era. It is the ultimate 'legacy system', and it was always 'over-specified' for the UK's needs, even in the Cold War. But then, as now, it gave the UK what it needed at an affordable price. Alternative systems, without the redundancy that *Trident* represents for the UK, would be either inadequate or more expensive, or both. Unlike previous generations of the deterrent, *Trident* is unlikely to face technical obsolescence during the remainder of its service life. But it will not last for ever. Before the new submarines enter service it will be necessary to decide what will replace the *Trident* missiles themselves. It is likely to be a *Trident* derivative.

Britain's relationship with the United States is key to its nuclear posture. During the Cold War, the UK needed to influence American nuclear policy so far as it was able. Britain no longer needs the US nuclear umbrella to the extent it once did, but does still want to influence US policies regarding non-proliferation and arms control. Being a nuclear power itself makes Britain's voice to some extent more credible in Washington.

The British nuclear deterrent is independently controlled, but 'US-enabled.'[9] Nuclear policy is to a degree a hostage to US decisions. Fortunately, the US government appears willing to go on enabling the British nuclear force. American assurances about the nature and availability of an eventual *Trident* successor represent a remarkable long-term undertaking, which demonstrates at least one tangible benefit to the UK of the special relationship.[10] There is, however, a particular dichotomy. A principal rationale for the operationally independent deterrent has always been that it provides insurance against a withdrawal of the American nuclear guarantee from Europe. In that event, Britain could probably not rely on continued US support for its own capability. This is a compromise which Britain prefers not to address, though France, at much greater cost, does. The effects on the British *Trident* system of a breakdown in transatlantic relations would be long term rather than immediate.[11] But such a development would force the UK to reappraise the level of resources it is prepared to devote to remaining a nuclear-armed state.

Nuclear weapons remain a highly sensitive issue within the governing Labour Party. The commitment of the party leadership to the UK's nuclear status is clear. Disquiet in the ranks may not matter because the main opposition party also supports nuclear retention. Without mainstream political leadership the anti-nuclear case will go no further than scoring debating points. Public support for the nuclear deterrent remains strong, though not at the same level as during the Cold War. In devolved Scotland it is a different case. There is no sign that the 'Scottish question' and its implications for *Trident* have featured in the government's thinking, at least not publicly.[12] This is not surprising, as to acknowledge the relevance of the question would undermine the government's devolution policy and amount to an admission of the possibility of unintended consequences. But the nuclear deterrent, at least in its current locations, will be vitally affected by the future constitutional integrity of the UK.

In its December 2006 White Paper, the British government clearly sets out why it intends to retain nuclear weapons, and in what form. It is rather less clear on how nuclear deterrence will be conducted, other than reiterating the need for ambiguity and independent decision-making. In the absence of a clearly identified adversary or adversaries, this is unsurprising. Most of the White Paper's section on 'Nuclear Deterrence in the 21st Century' discusses the need for a deterrent (mainly an insurance against an uncertain future)[13] rather than the functioning of deterrence. The reduction of threats through non-proliferation is treated as a separate activity, however proud of its 'forward-leaning' stance the UK may be. Only cursory attention is paid to defence against nuclear weapons and their delivery systems (or deterrence by denial).

This does not represent a fully 'joined-up' approach to proliferation and deterrence. In 1993 Rifkind pointed out the 'paradox' of a reliance on nuclear weapons for war-prevention at the same time that the spread of nuclear weapons represented one of the most serious threats to international stability.[14] To some extent, British policy does try to reconcile the two. A policy of deterrence recognises that non-proliferation is an incomplete answer, while Britain adjusts its deterrent capability to make as many gestures as possible towards non-proliferation short of abandoning nuclear weapons altogether.

However, deterrence is not a complete solution either. In the second nuclear age deterrence is necessarily more uncertain, more diffuse and less reliable than during the Cold War. We are still obliged to think strategically[15] but in an environment that is more complex than the relatively simple, if terrifying, certainties of the first nuclear age. Deterrence needs to be more flexible and the deterrent, if it is to be credible, must be 'useable'. Cold-War deterrence accepted assured vulnerability, a regrettable necessity rather than a preferred choice. Today it is not clear that vulnerability is either necessary or desirable. To the extent that it may be unnecessary, vulnerability is certainly *not* desirable, given the incompleteness of both non-proliferation and deterrence as solutions to the gravest security challenges. Relative technological sophistication between *some* threats and *some* defences means that the latter's time, in some circumstances, may have come.

The UK perhaps needs its own 'strategic triad' – diplomacy, deterrence and defence ('D3'). Diplomacy, including non-proliferation and arms control should seek to prevent, reduce or eliminate severe threats to our security. Deterrence must dissuade those whom diplomatic tools cannot deal with fully. Defence (both active and passive) is needed to reinforce deterrence and, ultimately, to mitigate the effects of diplomatic and deterrence failure.

NOTES

Introduction

1   Nicholas Witney, 'British Nuclear Policy after the Cold War', *Survival*, vol. 36, no. 4, Winter 1994–95, p. 97.

2   *Statement on the Defence Estimates 1996*, Cm 3223 (London: The Stationery Office (TSO), May 1996): http://www.archive. official-documents.co.uk/document/ mod/defence/deffc.htm.

3   For example, *The Sunday Times* lead article, 7 January 2007: 'Revealed: Israel Plans Nuclear Strike on Iran', by Uzi Mahnaimi and Sarah Baxter.

4   Bagehot, 'A Ticking Bomb: The Future of Britain's Nuclear Deterrent', *The Economist*, 16 March 2006, p. 34.

5   *Strategic Defence Review*, Cm 3999 (London: TSO, July 1998), p. 17: http://www.mod. uk/NR/rdonlyres/65F3D7AC-4340-4119- 93A2-20825848E50E/0/sdr1998_complete. pdf.

6   Cm 3999, Supporting Essays, p. 5-1.

7   HC 986 House of Commons Defence Committee Eighth Report of Session 2005– 06, *The Future of the UK's Strategic Nuclear Deterrent: The Strategic Context* (London: TSO, 30 June 2006), p. 13: http://www. publications.parliament.uk/pa/cm200506/ cmselect/cmdfence/986/98602.htm.

8   *Delivering Security in a Changing World: Defence White Paper*, Cm 6041-I (London: TSO, December 2003), p. 9: http://www. mod.uk/NR/rdonlyres/051AF365-0A97-

4550-99C0-4D87D7C95DED/0/cm6041I_ whitepaper2003.pdf.

9   HC 986, p. 6.

10 *The Future of the United Kingdom's Nuclear Deterrent*, Cm 6994 (London: TSO, December 2006), p. 7: http://www. mod.uk/NR/rdonlyres/AC00DD79- 76D6-4FE3-91A1-6A56B03C092F/0/ DefenceWhitePaper2006_Cm6994.pdf.

11 The decision to acquire the *Polaris* submarine-launched system was taken in the early 1960s, and the decision to replace it with *Trident* was taken in the early 1980s.

12 The main sites being on the Clyde in Scotland and at Barrow-in-Furness, Derby, Aldermaston and Devonport in England.

13 Cm 6994, p. 7.

14 Tim Hare, 'Should the Decision on Trident Replacement be a Subject of Public and Parliamentary Debate?' in Ken Booth and Frank Barnaby, eds, *The Future of Britain's Nuclear Weapons: Experts Reframe the Debate* (Oxford: Oxford Research Group, March 2006), p. 68.

15 Cm 6041-I, p. 9. This statement is reiterated in Cm 6994, p. 12.

16 Overall numbers fell from about 65,000 in 1986 to around 20,000 by 2002. Tod Lindberg, 'Nuclear and Other Retaliation after Deterrence Fails' in Henry D. Sokolski, ed., *Getting MAD: Nuclear*

Mutual Assured Destruction, its Origins and Practice (Carlisle, PA: Strategic Studies Institute, 2004), p. 332.

17 Colin S. Gray, *The Second Nuclear Age* (Boulder, CO: Lynne Rienner, 1999), p. 25; Cm 6994, p. 5.

18 Michael Quinlan, 'The Future of Nuclear Weapons: Policy for Western Possessors', *International Affairs*, vol. 69, no. 3, May 1993, p. 487.

19 Cm 6994, p. 10.

Chapter One

1 In the early years of the nuclear age, the word 'atomic' was most commonly used. After the detonation of the first fusion ('thermonuclear') bombs in the 1950s, the word 'nuclear' became widespread, 'atomic' referring to the earlier fission weapons. However, 'nuclear' is today used to describe both fission and fusion weapons, and also nuclear reactors, both civil and military, all of which entail fission reactions.

2 For a full account of Britain's wartime role in the development of the first atomic bombs, see Margaret Gowing, *Britain and Atomic Energy 1939–1945* (London: Macmillan, 1964).

3 The story of the development of the first British bomb is told in the official history by Gowing, *Independence and Deterrence* (London: Macmillan, 1974) and in Brian Cathcart, *Test of Greatness* (London: John Murray, 1994).

4 Quinlan, 'The British Experience', in Sokolski, p. 263.

5 National Archives CAB 131/12 D(52)26, 17 June 1952. Reproduced in John Baylis, *Ambiguity and Deterrence: British Nuclear Strategy 1945–1964* (Oxford: Clarendon Press, 1996), Appendix 6.

6 Humphrey Wynn, *RAF Nuclear Deterrent Forces* (London: HMSO, 1994), chapter 21.

7 Baylis, *Ambiguity and Deterrence*, p. 260.

8 *Agreement for Cooperation on the Uses of Atomic Energy for Mutual Defence Purposes*, Cmnd 537 (London: HMSO, 1958): http://www.acronym.org.uk/docs/0406/MDA.pdf.

9 Claire Taylor and Tim Youngs, *The Future of the British Nuclear Deterrent*, House of Commons Library Research Paper 06/53 (London: House of Commons, 3 November 2006), p. 9: http://www.parliament.uk/commons/lib/research/rp2006/rp06-053.pdf.

10 Stocker, *Britain and Ballistic Missile Defence 1942–2002* (London: Frank Cass, 2004), p. 104; National Archives, AIR 8/2263 AUS (A) to PS to SofS, 1 June 1961.

11 The story of the *Polaris* programme is told in Peter Nailor, *The Nassau Connection* (London: HMSO, 1988).

12 Baylis, *Ambiguity and Deterrence*, p. 341.

13 National Archives DEFE 11/437 COS 1702/11/8/67 Annex A, 11 August 1967.

14 Stanley Orman, *Faith in G.O.D.S.: Stability in the Nuclear Age* (London: Brassey's, 1991), p. 35.

15 HC 986, p. 14. See also Stocker, *Britain and Ballistic Missile Defence*, pp. 148–50, and Lawrence Freedman, *Britain and Nuclear Weapons* (London: Macmillan, 1980), p. 47.

16 For a much fuller discussion of the significance of the Moscow ABM system, see Stocker, *Britain and Ballistic Missile Defence*, chapter 7, and Baylis, 'British Nuclear Doctrine: The "Moscow Criterion" and the Polaris Improvement Programme', *Contemporary British History*, vol. 19, no. 1, Spring 2005.

17 *Statement on the Defence Estimates 1983*, Cmnd 8951-I, vol. 1, p. 7.

18 Taylor and Youngs, *The Future of the British Nuclear Deterrent*, p. 13.

19 Len Scott, 'Labour and the Bomb: The First 80 Years', *International Affairs*, vol. 82, no. 4, July 2006, p. 690.

20 Gowing, *Independence and Deterrence*, vol. 2, pp. 499–500.

21 Peter Riddell, 'Nuclear Arms Will Keep Union Jack', *The Times*, 15 March 2006.

22 Cited in Freedman, 'British Nuclear Targeting', in Desmond Ball and Jeffrey Richelson, eds, *Strategic Nuclear Targeting* (Ithaca, NY: Cornell University Press, 1986), p. 114.

23 Freedman, *The Evolution of Nuclear Strategy*, 3rd edn (Basingstoke: Palgrave Macmillan, 2003), p. 296.

24 Avery Goldstein, *Deterrence and Security in the 21st Century: China, Britain and France and the Enduring Legacy of the Nuclear Revolution* (Stanford CA: Stanford University Press, 2000), p. 160.

25 Ian Clark, *Nuclear Diplomacy and the Special Relationship: Britain's Deterrent and America, 1957–1962* (Oxford: Clarendon Press, 1994), p. 389.

26 Freedman, *The Evolution of Nuclear Strategy*, p. 195; MoD, *The Future United Kingdom Strategic Nuclear Deterrent Force*, Defence Open Government Document 80/23, July 1908, para. 33.

27 Quinlan in evidence to the House of Commons Defence Committee, HC 986 Ev. 12.

28 Goldstein, *Deterrence and Security in the 21st Century*, p. 173.

29 Taylor and Youngs, *The Future of the British Nuclear Deterrent*, p. 11.

30 Robert S. Norris and Hans M. Kristensen, 'Nuclear Pursuits', *Bulletin of the Atomic Scientists*, September/October 2003, p. 71.

31 Freedman, 'British Nuclear Targeting', p. 117.

32 C.R. Hill, R.S. Pease, P.E. Peierls and J. Rotblat, *Does Britain Need Nuclear Weapons?* (London: British Pugwash Group, 1995), p. 25.

33 Christopher Watson, 'A Time to Phase Out the UK Nuclear Deterrent?', paper presented at Chatham House conference, Britain's Nuclear Weapons Debate, London, 10 July 2006.

34 Baylis, 'British Nuclear Doctrine', pp. 62–3.

35 MoD, *Trident and the Alternatives*, Defence Open Government Document 87/01, January 1987, pp. 3–4.

36 Taylor and Youngs, *The Future of the British Nuclear Deterrent*, p. 13.

37 MoD, *The United Kingdom Trident Programme*, Defence Open Government Document 82/1, March 1982, p. 6.

38 Defence Open Government Document 87/01, p. 1.

39 *Hansard*, 18 January 2005, Col.29WS.

40 Keith Hartley, 'The Economics of UK Nuclear Weapons Policy', *International Affairs*, vol. 82, no. 4, July 2006, p. 678.

41 *Hansard*, 10 February 2004, Col.1331W.

42 Malcolm Rifkind, 'The Role of Nuclear Weapons in UK Defence Strategy', *Brassey's Defence Yearbook 1994* (London: Brassey's, 1994, p. 30.

43 Norman Polmar, 'Strategic Submarine Progress', *U.S. Naval Institute Proceedings*, vol. 132, no. 10, October 2005, p. 85.

44 *Hansard*, 30 July 1998, Col.449.

45 Cm 3999, p. 19.

46 *Hansard*, 30 July 1998, Col.448.

47 Hill et al., *Does Britain Need Nuclear Weapons?*, p. 6.

48 Bruno Tertrais, *Nuclear Policies in Europe*, Adelphi Paper 327 (London: IISS–Oxford University Press, 1999), p. 18.

49 HC 986, p. 13.

50 Tertrais, *Nuclear Policies in Europe*, p. 32.

51 *Hansard*, 22 November 1991, Col.543.

52 Rifkind, 'The Role of Nuclear Weapons in UK Defence Strategy', pp. 31–2.

53 Cm 3999, p. 18.

54 Cm 6994, p. 23.

55 Michael Codner, 'Britain's Nuclear Deterrent: Keeping the Options Open', *RUSI Newsbrief*, vol. 25, no. 8, August 2005, p. 88.

56 HC 986, p. 13.

57 *Hansard*, 19 March 1998, Col.724.

58 Barnaby, 'What is Trident? The Facts and Figures of Britain's Nuclear Force' in Booth and Barnaby, p. 9.

59 For example, HC 986, p. 13.

60 MoD, *UK's Strategic Nuclear Deterrent*, Memorandum submitted to House

of Commons Defence Committee, 20 January 2006, Annex B, para. C.

[61] Taylor and Youngs, *The Future of the British Nuclear Deterrent*, p. 14.

[62] Ainslie, *The Future of the British Bomb* (London: WMD Awareness Programme, 2005), p. 89.

[63] *Hansard*, 30 July 1998, Col.449.

[64] HC 986, p. 8.

[65] Cm 6694, p. 12.

[66] For example, Cm 3999, p. 19; *The Future of the UK's Strategic Deterrent: government Response of the Committee's Eighth Report of Session 2006-6*, HC 1558, 26 July 2006, p. 3; *Hansard*: 8 March 2005, Col.421WH; 2 February 2004, Col.752W; 30 July 1998, Col.448.

[67] Cm 6694, pp.13, 23.

[68] Internal unclassified MoD briefing paper.

[69] MoD Directorate of Chemical, Biological, Radiological and Nuclear Policy 21-06-2005-094719-001, Freedom of Information response, 19 July 2005.

[70] HC 986, Ev. 36.

[71] Cm 3999, p. 5-2.

[72] Cm 6694, p. 5.

[73] Internal unclassified MoD briefing.

[74] Michael Clarke, 'Does My Bomb Look Big in This? Britain's Nuclear Choices After Trident', *International Affairs*, vol. 80, no. 1, January 2004, p. 53.

[75] Gray, 'An International "Norm" Against Nuclear Weapons? The British Case', *Comparative Strategy*, vol. 20, July 2001, p. 235.

[76] MoD, Memorandum, *UK's Strategic Nuclear Deterrent*, Annex C, para. 3.

[77] Codner, *Britain's Nuclear Deterrent*, p. 87.

[78] Cm 3999, p. 5-5.

[79] Cm 3999, Supporting Essay Five.

[80] Cm 5566, Vol. I, *The Strategic Defence Review: A New Chapter* (London: TSO, July 2002), p. 12.

Chapter Two

[1] Witney, 'British Nuclear Policy After the Cold War', pp. 108–9.

[2] Clarke, 'Does My Bomb Look Big in This?', p. 49.

[3] Keith Payne, *Deterrence in the Second Nuclear Age* (Lexington, KY: University Press of Kentucky, 1996); Gray, *The Second Nuclear Age*; Paul Bracken, 'The Second Nuclear Age', *Foreign Affairs*, vol. 79, no. 1, January/February 2000.

[4] David S. Yost, *The US and Nuclear Deterrence in Europe*, Adelphi Paper 326 (London: IISS–Oxford University Press, 1999), pp.14–18.

[5] Booth, 'Debating the Future of Trident: Who are the Real Realists?', in Booth and Barnaby, p. 79.

[6] Quinlan, 'Nuclear Weapons and the Abolition of War', *International Affairs*, vol. 67, no. 2, April 1991, p. 295.

[7] Josiane Gabel, 'The Role of U.S. Nuclear Weapons After September 11', *The Washington Quarterly*, vol. 28, no. 1, Winter 2004–05, p. 193.

[8] Gray, *Modern Strategy* (Oxford: Oxford University Press, 1999), p. 302.

[9] Gray, *The Second Nuclear Age*, p. 2.

[10] McGeorge Bundy, William J. Crowe and Sidney D. Drell, *Reducing Nuclear Danger* (New York: Council on Foreign Relations Press, 1993), p. 5.

[11] Gray, *Another Bloody Century: Future Warfare* (London: Weidenfeld & Nicolson, 2005), p. 276; Paul Rogers presentation at Chatham House conference, Britain's Nuclear Weapons Debate, London, 10 July 2006.

[12] Quinlan, *Thinking About Nuclear Weapons*, Whitehall Paper 41 (London: Royal United Services Institute, 1997), p. 19. Quinlan credits Sir Hermann Bondi with the original observation.

[13] Gray, *Modern Strategy*, p. 347.

[14] Julian Lewis, 'Nuclear Disarmament Versus Peace in the 21st Century', *RUSI*

Journal, vol. 151, no. 2, April 2006, pp. 50–54.

[15] HC 986, p. 25.

[16] Quinlan, 'The Future of United Kingdom Nuclear Weapons: Shaping the Debate', International Security, vol. 82, no. 4, July 2006, pp. 635–4.

[17] Ainslie, The Future of the British Bomb, p. 19.

[18] Michael MccGwire, 'Comfort Blanket or Weapon of War: What is Trident For?', International Affairs, vol. 82, no. 4, July 2006, p. 643.

[19] Booth, 'Debating the Future of Trident', p. 90.

[20] Cm 6994, p. 18.

[21] HC 1558, p. 4.

[22] HC 986, Ev.32.

[23] Hansard, 4 December 2006, Cols.23–24.

[24] For a recent examination of Russian strategic forces, see Henry Ivanov, 'Austere Deterrence', Jane's Defence Weekly, 3 May 2006, pp. 24–9.

[25] Gray, The Second Nuclear Age, p. 25.

[26] Cm 6994, p. 19.

[27] Clarke, 'Does My Bomb Look Big in This?', p. 56.

[28] T. Milne, H. Beach, J.L. Finney, S. Pease and J. Rotblat, An End to UK Nuclear Weapons (London: British Pugwash Group, 2002), p. 13.

[29] Quinlan, The Future of Deterrent Capability, p. 10; and T.V. Paul, 'Power, Influence and Nuclear Weapons' in T.V. Paul, Richard J. Harknett and James J. Wirtz, eds, The Absolute Weapon Revisited: Nuclear Arms and the Emerging International Order (Ann Arbor, MI: University of Michigan Press, 1998), p. 38.

[30] Paul Nitze, cited in Dennis M. Gormley, 'Securing Nuclear Obsolescence', Survival, vol. 48, no. 3, Autumn 2006, p. 131.

[31] Lewis, 'Nuclear Disarmament Versus Peace in the 21st Century', p. 53.

[32] Robert O'Neill, 'Weapons of the Underdog', Baylis and O'Neill, eds, Alternative Nuclear Futures: The Role of Nuclear Weapons in the Post-Cold War World (Oxford: Oxford University Press, 2000), p. 194; Codner, 'Britain's Nuclear Deterrent', p. 88.

[33] Smart, The Future of the British Nuclear Deterrent (London: Royal Institute of International Affairs, 1977), p. 5.

[34] Cm 6994, p. 20, para. 5.

[35] Quinlan, 'The Future of UK Nuclear Weapons', pp. 634–5.

[36] HC 1558, p. 4.

[37] MccGwire, 'The Rise and Fall of the NPT', International Affairs, vol. 81, no. 1, January 2005, p. 134.

[38] Goldstein, Deterrence and Security in the 21st Century, p. 57.

[39] Hansard, 4 December 2006, Col. 24.

[40] HC 986, p. 21.

[41] MccGwire, 'The Rise and Fall of the NPT', p. 137.

[42] Andy McSmith, 'Britain Will Remain US Poodle if Trident Replaced, Short Warns', Independent, 7 December 2005.

[43] Lewis Page and Rodric Braithwaite, 'Should Britain Renew the Trident Nuclear Deterrent?', Prospect, August 2006, p. 22.

[44] Greenpeace, Why Britain Should Stop Deploying Trident (London: Greenpeace, March 2006), p. 2.

[45] Memorandum submitted by British-American Security Information Council, HC 986, Ev. 116.

[46] Caroline Lucas, 'Is There a Sound Political Rationale for the UK Retaining Its Nuclear Weapons?', Booth and Barnaby, p. 23.

[47] George W. Bush, Message to the Congress of the United States, 14 June 2004: http://www.whitehouse.gov/news/releases/2004/06/print/20040614-16.html.

[48] Andrew Dorman, 'Prestige Purchase', The World Today, vol. 62, no. 4, May 2006, p. 14. See also Quinlan's comments to the House of Commons Defence Committee, HC 982, Ev. 12.

[49] Quinlan, The Future of Deterrent Capability, p. 9.

[50] Freedman, 'Great Powers, Vital Interests and Nuclear Weapons', Survival, vol. 36, no.4, Winter 1994–95, p. 46.

[51] Yost, 'France's Evolving Nuclear Strategy', Survival, vol. 47, no. 3, Autumn 2005, p. 134.

[52] Tertrais, Memorandum for House of Commons Defence Committee, HC 986, Ev. 82.

53 Quinlan, *The Future of Deterrent Capability*, p. 11.
54 Tony Blair, interview with Jeremy Paxman, BBC *Newsnight*, 20 April 2005.
55 *Hansard*, 22 November 2006, Col. 540.
56 David Clark, 'The Blairite Love Affair With The Bomb Will Cost Britain Dear', *Guardian*, 1 November 2005.
57 Conservative Research Department, *The Campaign Guide* (London: The Conservative Party, 31 March 2005).
58 Michael Portillo, 'Does Britain Need Nuclear Missiles? No. Scrap Them', *The Times*, 19 June 2005.
59 Nick Brown, 'UK To Begin Trident Replacement Debate', *Jane's Defence Weekly*, 1 February 2006, p. 7; Riddell, 'Poll Shows Gender Gap Over Renewal of Nuclear Deterrent', *The Times*, 13 December 2006.
60 A 1996 advisory opinion delivered by the International Court of Justice and a 2004 opinion by two members of Matrix Chambers in London.
61 Steven Haines letter published in *RUSI Defence Systems*, Winter/Spring 2005–06, p. 22; Nick Grief and Steven Haines, 'Is Britain's Continued Possession and Threatened Use of Nuclear Weapons Illegal?', in Booth and Barnaby, eds, pp. 41–57.
62 For a discussion of the controversy surrounding the demise of the ABM Treaty, see Stocker, *Britain and Ballistic Missile Defence*, pp. 224–6.
63 MccGwire, 'Comfort Blanket or Weapon of War', p. 640.
64 Lucas, 'Is There A Sound Political Rationale...', p. 25.
65 HC 986, Ev. 23.
66 Grief and Haines, 'Is Britain's Continued Possession and Threatened Use of Nuclear Weapons Illegal?', Booth and Barnaby, p. 41.
67 For a fuller (and more expert) examination of the implication of the NPT for the current debate, see the evidence submitted to the House of Commons Defence Committee by Quinlan, HC 986, Ev. 65.
68 Cm 6994, p. 7.
69 Bruce Blair, cited in Ainslie, *The Future of the British Bomb*, p. 21.
70 HC 986, Ev. 115.
71 Ainslie, *The Future of the British Bomb*, p. 22.
72 Professor Shaun Gregory, evidence to House of Commons Defence Committee HC 986, Ev. 24.
73 For a fuller examination of the cost issue, see Hartley, 'The Economics of UK Nuclear Weapons Policy', pp. 675–84.
74 Hare, 'Should the Decision on Trident Replacement be a Subject of Public and Parliamentary Debate?', p. 67.
75 Michael Meacher MP in *Hansard*, 4 December 2006, Col.29.
76 Cm 6994, p. 7.
77 Codner, 'Britain's Nuclear Deterrent', p. 87.
78 Hill et al., *Does Britain Need Nuclear Weapons?*, p. 53.
79 MccGwire, 'Comfort Blanket or Weapon of War', p. 646.
80 Mary Midgley, 'Can the Retention of British Nuclear Weapons be Justified Ethically in Today's World?', Booth and Barnaby, pp. 74–5.
81 Gregory, Evidence to the House of Commons Defence Committee, HC 986, Ev. 19.
82 *NATO's Nuclear Fact Sheets* (Brussels: NATO, 2006), p. 5.
83 Gray, 'An International "Norm" Against Nuclear Weapons? The British Case', pp. 231, 233.
84 Cm 3999, p. 17,
85 Smart, *The Future of the British Nuclear Deterrent*, p. 6.

Chapter Three

1   Gray, *Maintaining Effective Deterrence* (Carlisle, PA: Strategic Studies Institute, 2003), p. 1.
2   Remarks at IISS–Oxford University conference on Challenging Deterrence, Oxford, 14–16 December 2006.
3   Quinlan, *Thinking About Nuclear Weapons*, p. 12.
4   Remarks at IISS–Oxford University conference on Challenging Deterrence, Oxford, 14–16 December 2006.
5   Freedman conceptualises it a little differently. For him, deterrence and compellence are both coercive strategies, the former to prevent and the latter to force, certain actions. Freedman, *Deterrence* (Cambridge: Polity Press, 2004), pp. 26–7.
6   Wyn Bowen, 'Deterrence and Asymmetry: Non-State Actors and Mass Casualty Terrorism', in Ian Kenyon and John Simpson, eds, *Deterrence and the New Global Security Environment* (Abingdon: Taylor and Francis, 2006), p. 51.
7   Freedman, *Deterrence*, p. 29.
8   The best comprehensive history of nuclear deterrence theories is Freedman, *The Evolution of Nuclear Strategy*. See also Fred Kaplan, *The Wizards of Armageddon* (New York: Simon & Schuster, 1983); Freedman, *The Revolution in Strategic Affairs*, Adelphi Paper 318 (London: IISS–Oxford University Press, 1998), p. 20.
9   Gray, *Maintaining Effective Deterrence*, p. 11.
10 Payne, 'The Nuclear Posture Review and Deterrence for a New Age', *Comparative Strategy*, vol. 23, 2004, p. 411.
11 Robert G. Joseph, 'Nuclear Deterrence and Regional Proliferators', *The Washington Quarterly*, vol. 20, no. 3, Summer 1997, p. 169.
12 Clarke, 'Does My Bomb Look Big in This?', p. 57; Hill et al., *Does Britain Need Nuclear Weapons?*, p. 58; Andrew J. Goodpaster, 'Nuclear Roles in the Post-Cold War World', reprint of second report of the Steering Committee for the Project on Eliminating Weapons of Mass Destruction, *The Washington Quarterly*, vol. 20, no. 3, Summer 1997, p. 164; Canberra Commission on the Elimination of Nuclear Weapons, see Freedman, 'Eliminators, Marginalists and the Politics of Disarmament', in Baylis and O'Neill, p. 65.
13 Gray, *Modern Strategy*, p. 338.
14 Ibid., p. 328; Quinlan, *Thinking About Nuclear Weapons*, pp. 18–19.
15 Payne, 'The Nuclear Posture Review and Deterrence', p. 415.
16 Cited in Payne 'The Nuclear Posture Review: Setting the Record Straight', *The Washington Quarterly*, vol. 28, no. 3, Summer 2005, p. 135.
17 Cm 3999, p. 5-1.
18 Remark made at Wilton Park conference, 'The Future of Nuclear Deterrence in the North Atlantic Alliance', 12–15 October 2006.
19 Evidence submitted to the House of Commons Defence Committee, HC 986, Ev. 94.
20 Chemical and biological weapons are prohibited by international treaties, the 1993 Chemical Weapons Convention and the 1972 Biological and Toxin Weapons Convention, respectively. See HC 407 House of Commons Foreign Affairs Committee Eighth Report, Session 1999–2000, *Weapons of Mass Destruction* (London: TSO, 25 July 2000), Annexes III and IV: http://www.publications.parliament.uk/pa/cm199900/cmselect/cmfaff/407/40702.htm.
21 Ibid.
22 Lewis Dunn, *Beyond the Cold War Nuclear Legacy: Offense–Defense and the Role of Nuclear Deterrence* (Paris: Institut Français des Relations Internationales, 2001), p. 29.
23 Payne, *Deterrence in the Second Nuclear Age*, pp. 84–5.
24 Wing Commander D.A. Stamp (RAF), 'Does the United Kingdom Require a Strategic Deterrent Capability Post-2030?', *Royal Air Force Air Power Review*, vol. 9, no. 1, Spring 2006, p. 9.

25 Cited in Tertrais, *Nuclear Policies in Europe*, p. 40.

26 Yost, 'New Approaches to Deterrence in Britain, France and the United States', *International Affairs*, vol. 81, no. 1, January 2005, p. 85.

27 HC 986 Ev.94.

28 Freedman, *The Revolution in Strategic Affairs*, p. 47.

29 *Hansard*, 19 October 2005, Col.841.

30 Freedman, *The Evolution of Nuclear Strategy*, p. 456.

31 For a much more comprehensive examination of nuclear terrorism, see Robin M. Frost, *Nuclear Terrorism After 9/11*, Adelphi Paper 378 (London: IISS–Taylor & Francis, December 2005). Frost is sceptical about the likelihood of nuclear-armed terrorism; William C. Potter, *Trends in U.S. Nuclear Policy* (Paris: Institut Français des Relations Internationales, 2005), p. 13.

32 Daniel Whiteneck, 'Deterring Terrorists: Thoughts on a Framework', *The Washington Quarterly*, vol. 28, no. 3, Summer 2005, p. 187.

33 Anna M. Pluta and Peter D. Zimmerman, 'Nuclear Terrorism: A Disheartening Dissent', *Survival*, vol. 48, no. 2, Summer 2006, p. 65.

34 HC 986, p. 24.

35 HC 986, Ev. 43.

36 Frost, *Nuclear Terrorism After 9/11*, p. 70.

37 Cm 6994, p. 19; *Hansard*, 4 December 2006, Col.24.

38 Quinlan, Evidence to House of Commons Defence Committee HC 986, Ev. 1.

39 NATO, *The Alliance's Strategic Concept* (Washington DC: NATO, April 1999), p. 20.

40 Freedman, *The Revolution in Strategic Affairs*, p. 51.

41 Kenneth N. Waltz, *The Spread of Nuclear Weapons: More May Be Better*, Adelphi Paper 171 (London: IISS, 1981), p. 24.

42 Payne, *Deterrence in the Second Nuclear Age*, p. 136.

43 Clarke, 'Does My Bomb Look Big in This?', p. 55.

44 Quinlan, 'The British Experience', p. 274.

45 Wirtz, 'Beyond Bipolarity: Prospects for Nuclear Stability After the Cold War', in Paul et al., *The Absolute Weapon Revisited*, p. 140.

46 Freedman, *Deterrence*, p. 18.

47 Quinlan, *Thinking About Nuclear Weapons*, p. 15.

48 Payne, *Fallacies of Cold War Deterrence and a New Direction* (Lexington, KY: University Press of Kentucky, 2001), p. 193.

49 Gray, *Modern Strategy*, p. 315.

50 Quinlan, *Thinking About Nuclear Weapons*, p. 16.

51 Lee Butler 'At the End of the Journey: The Risks of Cold War Thinking in a New Era', *International Affairs*, vol. 82, no. 4, July 2006, p. 769.

52 Lindberg, 'Nuclear and Other Retaliation After Deterrence Fails', p. 326.

53 Payne, 'The Nuclear Posture Review: Setting the Record Straight', p. 144.

54 Excerpts available at: http://www.globalsecurity.org/wmd/library/policy/dod/npr.htm. See also, David McDonough, *Nuclear Superiority: The 'New Triad' and the Evolution of Nuclear Strategy*, Adelphi Paper 383 (London: IISS–Oxford University Press, 2006).

55 For example, Drell et al., 'A Strategic Choice: New Bunker Busters Versus Nonproliferation', *Arms Control Today*, vol. 33, no. 2, March 2003, p. 9.

56 Bryan L. Fearey et al. 'An Analysis of Reduced Collateral Damage Nuclear Weapons', *Comparative Strategy*, vol. 22, 2003, p. 313.

57 HC 986, Ev. 26.

58 Freedman, *The Revolution in Strategic Affairs*, p. 39.

59 Bowen, p. 47.

60 Cited in Payne, *Fallacies of Cold War Deterrence*, p. 14.

61 Payne, *Deterrence in the Second Nuclear Age*, p. 131.

62 Freedman, *Revolution in Strategic Affairs*, p. 34.

63 Payne, *Fallacies of Cold War Deterrence*, p. 91.

64 Payne, *Deterrence in the Second Nuclear Age*, p. 34.

65 O'Neill, 'Weapons of the Underdog', in Baylis and O'Neill, p. 191.

66 Stephen J. Cimbala, 'Nuclear Weapons in the Twenty-First Century: From Simplicity to Complexity', *Defense and Security Analysis*, vol. 21, no. 3, September 2005, p. 270.

67 Philip Bobbitt, *The Shield of Achilles: War, Peace and the Course of History* (London: Allen Lane, 2002), p. 218.

68 Gray, *Another Bloody Century*, p. 289.

69 Payne, *Deterrence in the Second Nuclear Age*, p. 17.

70 Cm 6994, p. 18.

71 NATO, *The Alliance's Strategic Concept*, p. 20.

72 Goldstein, *Deterrence and Security in the 21st Century*, p. 49.

73 Quinlan, 'Deterrence and Deterability', in Kenyon and Simpson, p. 5.

74 Cm 6994, p. 18.

75 Bundy et al., *Reducing Nuclear Danger*, p. 82; Milne et al., *An End to UK Nuclear Weapons*, p. 31.

76 Tertrais, *Nuclear Policies in Europe*, p. 43.

77 Rifkind, 'The Role of Nuclear Weapons in UK Defence Strategy', p. 24.

78 Rogers, 'Big Boats and Bigger Skimmers: Determining Britain's Role in the Long War', *International Affairs*, vol. 82, no. 4, July 2006, p. 653.

79 For a fuller dismissal of the attraction of a no-first-use policy, see Quinlan, *Thinking About Nuclear Weapons*, pp. 50–54.

80 *NATO's Nuclear Fact Sheets*, p. 4.

81 Cm 3999, p. 5-11.

82 Remarks made at IISS–Oxford University conference *Challenging Deterrence*, Oxford, 14–16 December 2006.

83 Cm 3999, p. 17; Cm 6994, p. 7.

84 Henry S. Rowen, 'Introduction' in Sokolski, p. 8.

85 Quinlan, 'Aspiration, Realism and Practical Policy', in Baylis and O'Neill, p. 53.

86 Cm 6994, p. 18.

87 Quinlan, *Thinking About Nuclear Weapons*, p. 78.

88 Cm 6994, p. 14.

89 NATO, *The Alliance's Strategic Concept*, p. 20.

90 For a discussion of virtual deterrence, see Baylis 'Nuclear Weapons, Prudence and Morality: The Search for a "Third Way"', in Baylis and O'Neill, pp. 81–4.

91 Cm 6994, pp. 21, 27.

92 Yost, 'New Approaches to Deterrence', p. 99.

93 David S. McDonough, *Nuclear Superiority: The 'New Triad' and the Evolution of Nuclear Strategy*, Adelphi Paper 383 (London: IISS–Taylor & Francis, 2006), p. 10.

94 Freedman, *Deterrence*, p. 39.

95 Joseph, 'Nuclear Deterrence and Regional Proliferators', p. 170.

96 For the full story of British attitudes and policies towards missile defences, see Stocker, *Britain and Ballistic Missile Defence*.

97 Cm 6994, p. 21.

98 Gray, *The Second Nuclear Age*, p. 98.

99 Cimbala, 'Nuclear Weapons in the Twenty-First Century', p. 273.

100 Aaron Karp, 'The New Indeterminacy of Deterrence and Missile Defence', in Kenyon and Simpson, p. 64.

101 Bobbitt, *The Shield of Achilles*, p. 685.

102 Payne, *Deterrence in the Second Nuclear Age*, p. 143.

103 Tertrais, *Nuclear Policies in Europe*, p. 38.

104 Yost, 'New Approaches to Deterrence', p. 105.

105 Stocker, *Britain and Ballistic Missile Defence*, chapters 9 and 10. Little has changed since 2003 as attention has been on the future of the nuclear deterrent.

106 For example, remarks by Jan Lodal, a former US defence official cited in Payne, *Deterrence in the Second Nuclear Age*, p. 41.

107 Gray, *Modern Strategy*, p. 325.

108 For extended discussions of the reliability of deterrence, see Payne, *Deterrence in the Second Nuclear Age* and *Fallacies of Cold War Deterrence*; Gray, *The Second Nuclear Age*, pp. 88–91.

109 Freedman, *Deterrence*, p. 29.

110 Payne, 'The Nuclear Posture Review: Setting the Record Straight', p. 139.

111 Cm 6994, p. 17.

112 Gray, 'The Reformation of Deterrence: Moving On', *Comparative Strategy*, vol. 22, 2003, p. 441.

Chapter Four

1 John Deutch, 'A Nuclear Posture For Today', *Foreign Affairs*, vol. 84, no.1, January/February 2005, p. 51.

2 For example, Jonathan Schell, 'The Folly of Arms Control', *Foreign Affairs*, vol. 79, no. 5, September/October 2000, p. 23.

3 Cm 6994, p. 8.

4 Bobbitt, *The Shield of Achilles*, p. 683.

5 Michael Krepon, *Cooperative Threat Reduction, Missile Defense, and the Nuclear Future* (New York: Palgrave Macmillan, 2003), p. 169.

6 Gray, *The Second Nuclear Age*, p. 98.

7 Kenyon and Simpson, *Deterrence and the New Global Security Environment*, p. 19.

8 HC 407, p. 28.

9 Gray, *The Second Nuclear Age*, p. 59.

10 For example, William Walker, *Weapons of Mass Destruction and International Order*, Adelphi Paper 370 (London: IISS–Oxford University Press, 2004), p. 6.

11 MccGwire, 'Comfort Blanket or Weapon of War', p. 640.

12 HC 986, Ev. 93.

13 Remarks at IISS–Oxford University conference on *Challenging Deterrence* Oxford, 14–16 December 2006.

14 George H. Questor, 'The Unavoidable Importance of Nuclear Weapons', in Baylis and O'Neill, p. 32.

15 Cm 3999, p. 5-9.

16 Cm 6994, p. 7.

17 MoD and Foreign and Commonwealth Office, *The Future of the United Kingdom's Nuclear Deterrent*, Fact Sheet 3.

18 Lewis, 'Nuclear Disarmament Versus Peace in the 21st Century', p. 53.

19 Quinlan, 'Aspiration, Realism and Practical Policy', p. 52.

20 Malcolm Chalmers and William Walker, *Uncharted Waters: The UK, Nuclear Weapons and the Scottish Question* (Phantassie: The Tuckwell Press, 2001), pp. 86–7.

21 Cm 6994, p. 13.

22 Freedman, 'Eliminators, Marginalists and Disarmament', p. 59.

23 Gray, *The Second Nuclear Age*, p. 106.

24 Chalmers and Walker, *Uncharted Waters*, p. 86.

25 Cm 6994, Annex A.

26 Cm 6994, p. 30.

27 Deutch, 'A Nuclear Posture for Today', p. 58.

28 For good reviews of the PSI, see Joel Doolin, 'The Proliferation Security Initiative: Cornerstone of a New International Norm', *Naval War College Review*, vol. 59, no. 2, Spring 2006, and Mark J. Valencia, *The Proliferation Security Initiative*, Adelphi Paper 376 (London: IISS–Oxford University Press, 2005).

29 Mark Fitzpatrick, 'Weapons Watch', *The World Today*, vol. 62, no. 2, February 2006, p. 11.

30 Walker, *WMD and International Order*, p. 74.

31 HC 986, Ev. 62.

32 Atomic Weapons Establishment, *AWE Annual Report 2004/5* (Aldermaston: AWE, 2005), p. 11.

33 For a full examination of the Libyan case, see Bowen, *Libya and Nuclear Proliferation: Stepping Back From the Brink*, Adelphi Paper 380 (London: IISS–Taylor & Francis, 2006).

34 Iran's WMD programmes are examined at length in IISS, *Iran's Strategic Weapons Programmes: A Net Assessment* (London: IISS, 2005).

35 Wade L. Huntley, 'Rebels Without a Cause: North Korea, Iran and the NPT', *International Affairs*, vol. 82, no. 4, July 2006, p. 732.

36 Scott D. Sagan and Waltz, *The Spread of Nuclear Weapons: A Debate Renewed*, 2nd edn (New York: W.W. Norton & Co., 2003), p. 3.

37 Bobbitt, *The Shield of Achilles*, p. 218.

38 Gray, *The Second Nuclear Age*, p. 82; Fearey et al., 'An Analysis of Reduced Collateral Damage Nuclear Weapons', p. 321.

39 HC 407, p. 39.

40 Schell, 'The Folly of Arms Control', p. 41.

Chapter Five

1 Cm 6994, p. 26.

2 Cm 6994, Annex B.

3 Dorman, 'Prestige Purchase', p. 13; Willett, 'Questions for the Debate', p. 54.

4 Smart, *The Future of the British Nuclear Deterrent*. Smart's conclusion was confirmed by the MoD three years later: Defence Open Government Document 80/23, p. 21.

5 HC 1558, para. 22.

6 Quinlan, *The Future of Deterrent Capability for Medium-Sized Western Powers*, p. 13.

7 Cm 6994, p. 22.

8 Cm 6994, p. 25.

9 Cm 6994, p. 39.

10 See also Clarke, 'Does My Bomb Look Big in This?', p. 50; Willett, 'Questions for the Debate', p. 55; Quinlan, 'The Future of United Kingdom Nuclear Weapons', p. 635; Hare, HC 986, Ev. 37; RUSI in HC 986, Ev. 70.

11 Taylor and Youngs, *The Future of the British Nuclear Deterrent*, p. 39.

12 Cm 6994, p. 11.

13 HC 986, p. 31.

14 Cm 6994, p. 12.

15 Cm 6994, p. 26.

16 Polmar, 'Strategic Submarine Progress', p. 86.

17 Cm 6994, p. 31; the exchange of letters on the subject between Blair and Bush is available at: www.pm.gov.uk/output/Page10657.asp.

18 Ainslie, *The Future of the British Bomb*, p. 33.

19 Cm 6994, p. 12.

20 Cm 6994, p. 5.

21 HC 1558, p. 7.

22 Cm 6994, p. 26.

23 For a good summary of the role and operation of AWE, see House of Commons Defence Committee Fourth Report of Session 2006–07, HC 59, *The Future of the UK's Strategic Nuclear Deterrent: The Manufacturing and Skills Base* (London: TSO, 12 December 2006), pp. 32–5: http://www.publications.parliament.uk/pa/cm200607/cmselect/cmdfence/59/59.pdf.

24 For details, see: www.globalsecurity.org/wmd/systems/rrw.htm.

25 Bill Sweetman, 'Nuclear Family Planning: Fewer, Smaller and Safer Warheads for Future Generation', *Jane's International Defence Review*, January 2006, p. 62.

26 See HC 59, p. 38.

27 Cm 6994, p. 13.

28 Until 1998, submarines usually deployed with 60 warheads (*Hansard*, 30 July 1998, Col.449). Thereafter, submarines on patrol carried fewer than 16 missiles, including some configured for the single-warhead sub-strategic role.

29 Cm 6994, p. 9.

30 *Hansard*, 4 December 2006, Col.22. It is interesting to note that the 25-year life apparently runs from the time the submarine is launched, rather than when it enters service.

31 *Hansard*, 30 June 2004, Col.358W.

32 Cm 6041-I, para.3.11.

33 HC 1558, p. 8.

34 Cm 6994, p. 10.

35 Ibid.

36 For example, Memorandum from the British American Security Information Council, HC 986, Ev.120.

37 HC 986, p. 33; HC 59, p. 12.

38 John F. Schank et al., *The United Kingdom's Nuclear Submarine Industrial Base* (Santa Monica CA: RAND Corporation, 2005).

39 Ibid., vol. 2, p. 8; HC 59, p. 16.

40 *Jane's Defence Weekly*, 30 August 2006, p. 13.

41 For an update on the *Astute* programme, see Richard Scott 'Back from the Brink', *Jane's Defence Weekly*, 22 March 2006, pp. 34–7.

42 Author conversation with MoD official, August 2006.

43 Cited in Hartley, 'The Economics of UK Nuclear Weapons Policy', p. 683.

44 Cited in Richard Scott, 'Can UK Nuclear Submarine Industry Retain Critical Mass', *Jane's Navy International*, July/August 2006, p. 14.

45 Murray Easton, 'Future Submarines', *RUSI Defence Systems*, vol. 9, no. 2, Autumn 2006, pp. 44–6.

46 HC 59, pp. 9–10 contain a good summary of the entire supporting infrastructure.

47 HC 986, Ev. 10.

48 Defence Open Government Document 80/23, p. 21.

49 Cm 6994, pp.25–6.

50 HC 986, Ev. 39.

51 HC 986, Ev.141.

52 *Jane's Defence Weekly*, 21 September 2005, p. 13.

53 The Royal Navy's first SSN, HMS *Dreadnought*, had a US-supplied reactor pending development of a British plant for later boats. More recently, some American expertise has been used to get the *Astute* programme back on track.

54 Willett, 'Astute, Trident and SSGN: Land Attack for the Royal Navy Submarine Service', *RUSI Defence Systems*, vol. 8, no. 1, Summer 2005, p. 106.

55 Cm 6994, p. 26.

56 Hartley, 'The Economics of UK Nuclear Weapons Policy', p. 679. The prime minister said in the House of Commons that the *Vanguard*-class cost £14bn in today's prices. He presumably meant the cost of the original *Trident* programme as a whole, of which the submarines represented about 29%.

57 Author conversation with MoD official, August 2006.

58 Parliamentary Office of Science and Technology *The Nuclear Energy Option in the UK*, Postnote no. 208, December 2003, p. 1.

59 J.N. Fradgley, *Nuclear Energy: Threat or Opportunity?*, Seaford House Papers (Shrivenham: UK Defence Academy, 2005), p. 217.

60 Fradgley, *Nuclear Energy*, p. 225.

61 The Scottish question was examined in Chalmers and Walker, *Uncharted Waters*. Most of their analysis remains entirely pertinent today, and this short section draws extensively upon it.

62 *Sunday Telegraph*, 27 November 2006.

63 Chalmers and Walker, *Uncharted Waters*, p. 89.

64 Ibid., chapter 5.

65 Richard Scott, 'Can UK Nuclear Submarine Industry Retain Critical Mass?', p. 18.

66 HC 986, p. 41.

Conclusion

1 Ivo Daalder, 'What Vision for the Nuclear Future?', *The Washington Quarterly*, vol. 18, no. 2, Spring 1995, p. 139.

2 *Hansard,* 4 December 2006, Col.21.

3 Booth, 'Debating the Future of Trident', in Booth and Barnaby, p. 90.

4 Chalmers and Walker, *Uncharted Waters*, p. 103.

5 HC 986, Ev. 80.

6 Cm 6994, p. 5.

7 Robert Fox, 'Trident: The Done Deal', *New Statesman*, 13 June 2005, p. 19; Willett, 'Questions for the Debate on the Future of the UK Strategic Deterrent', *RUSI Journal*, vol. 150, no. 6, December 2005, p. 55; Taylor and Youngs, *The Future of the British Nuclear Deterrent*, p. 38.

8 Cm 6994, p. 7.

9 HC 986, Ev. 81.

10 Cm 6994, p. 31.

11 Hare, 'Should the Decision on Trident Replacement be a Subject of Public and Parliamentary Debate?', p. 67; HC 986, Ev. 35.

12 Tony Blair is 'not prepared to engage in that hypothesis', *Hansard,* 4 December 2006, Col.35.

13 Cm 6994, p. 18.

14 Rifkind, 'The Role of Nuclear Weapons in UK Defence Strategy', p. 34.

15 Gray, *The Second Nuclear Age*, p. 120.